BAX: BEST AMERICAN EXPERIMENTAL WRITING

Series Editors Seth Abramson and Jesse Damiani

Managing Editor Michael Martin Shea

BAX 2016

Guest Editors Charles Bernstein and Tracie Morris

BAX 2014
Guest Editor Cole Swensen

BAX 2015
Guest Editor Douglas Kearney

BAX

Guest Editors | *Charles Bernstein and Tracie Morris*
Series Editors | *Seth Abramson and Jesse Damiani*
Managing Editor | *Michael Martin Shea*

BEST AMERICAN
EXPERIMENTAL
WRITING

2016

Wesleyan University Press
Middletown, Connecticut

Wesleyan University Press

Middletown CT 06459

www.wesleyan.edu/wespress

© 2016 Wesleyan University Press

Manufactured in the United States of America

Designed by Mindy Basinger Hill

Typeset in Minion Pro

Hardcover ISBN: 978-0-8195-7673-6

Paperback ISBN: 978-0-8195-7674-3

Ebook ISBN: 978-0-8195-7675-0

5   4   3   2   1

Contents

Digital-only contributions to BAX 2016 *can be found at: bax.site.wesleyan.edu.*

CHARLES BERNSTEIN AND TRACIE MORRIS
Guest Editors' Introduction

America is an experiment.

Thomas Jefferson thought that there needed to be a rebellion against the existing government every twenty years, even if, as he recognized, some of those rebellions were fueled more by ignorance than a desire for liberty. During this election year, we may well ask if all rebellions are equally valued, but every generation certainly needs a revolution of the word. The initial rebellions of L=A=N=G=U=A=G=E, the Black Arts Movement, and Hip Hop are already two generations behind us. Since that time, American poetry's mainstreams have absorbed some of the stylistic manners of these movements but not the burning desire for unpredictability, development, and change. What the mainstreams have absorbed is some of the technique but not the motivation. A style that was cutting edge twenty years ago isn't going to cut it now. A style that is cutting edge right now won't be so for long.

Art isn't easy. It's not just that we need a revolution in style but also a revolution in audience, distribution, circulation, performance, perception, and, indeed, motivation. These revolutions are never a question of being marked as ahead of the times—that is the problem with the label *avant-garde*, with its flamboyant promise of "being out front." Rather, the issue is staying in and with the times and not letting the times drown us. In editing this collection, we looked for works that refuse to be sunk by a faddist, temporal undertow.

All the standard terms for inventiveness in the arts are vexing, even when well intentioned. *Experiment* can suggest that the focus is on the work-product or test results, despite the fact that writing that is open to new possibilities is more likely to be aesthetically accomplished than work that closes off such possibilities. *Avant-garde* often evokes a hermetically sealed tradition hobbled by its own triumphalism. We need avant-garde literary history to revolutionize overly narrow lineages and to acknowledge that the revolution of the word was fomented by writers who operated both inside and outside the cultural, ethnic, religious, or racial mainstreams. Which is to say, along with a host of literary scholars, artists, and anthologists from the past few decades, avant-garde history has not always acknowledged its innovators. At the same time, many of those hostile to what they call avant-garde poetry gerrymander the term to suit their foregone biases against it.

Rather than saying *avant-garde*, we say *en garde*: wake up, poetry is about to begin!

In 2015, as for a hundred years before, innovative poetry continued to be controversial. Of course, there is much to be critical of in poetry's multitude of iterations, and most practitioners of anything remotely resembling the experimental are quick to make a wide range of criticism, since this is a group of unlike-minded individuals. But all the hoopla suggests that what's innovative is, paradoxically, at the vital center of contemporary poetics and that its symbolic constructions are therefore subject to the most virulent scrutiny and worthwhile critique.

But, yes, the innovative needs to change, to *re*volve, or else it will become nothing more than the fashion and design wing of officially sanctioned verse culture. Or you could say, all the en-garde is is an indication of change.

The exploration of identities has always been at the center of radical and exploratory poetry. Indeed, a difference between official verse culture and its opposites can be defined as one between work that assumes a fixed identity and work that forges new identity constructions. In this sense, identity is a space for exploration, invention, re-creation, and experimentation. No one group has, or has ever had, a monopoly on this. The source of the most provocative American poetics is the collective linguistic expression of all groups refracted into culturally specific works.

In the brutal calculus of official verse culture, it is claimed that identity is erased in "experimental" writing. But one person's erasure may be another's path to freedom, just as one person's experimental diversion may be another's fate. We favor thick description over thin convention, the discovered over the assumed. Identity is a process and an intersection: it unfolds as it is veiled. We are not against writing from one's identity; rather, we seek a more robust engagement with identity than is often found in conventional writing or narrowly defined experimental writing collections. We wanted to open up this book to a range of voices that, we hope, enrich each other by being in the same volume.

We edited this book in collaboration with the two series editors. We were asked to choose forty-five selections from work either published in 2015 or not yet published. We further created our own, stricter criteria to bring more voices into this conversation: we omitted current or recent students or colleagues at institutions where we have primarily worked and authors published in the first two *BAX* anthologies (which meant leaving out much work that we admire). We also excluded anyone whose poetic work was published by the early 1990s. Since so many poets from this generation are continuing to do some of the best experimental work around, we felt we needed to make room here for new writers (or anyway, newer ones). But we didn't want to leave out the older generations entirely, so we have included select works by major figures working outside genres for which they are known. We also didn't select any translations, as we felt including just a few would fall woefully short of representing the vibrancy of poetry written around the world. We'd like to see a book like this one just of translations, emphasizing also new approaches to the art. In addition to our forty-five selections, the series editors made fifteen selections. The remainder of the works in the anthology were chosen from submitted manuscripts; these were picked by the series editors and us. We hope that this mix makes for a strong volume and contributes to the development of the *BAX* series.

Although we are happy with the resulting volume, the necessary compromises among the four editors, and the inevitable space limitations, has meant that we were disappointed we could not include many outstanding works. We especially want to express our appreciation to the many extraordinary poets who submitted work we were unable to include as well as our colleagues, students and friends. We could not do what we do without our intersecting and ever-expanding communities.

Editors of anthologies committed to the best of conventional writing are likely to reject work because they have never seen anything like it before. In contrast, we tend to reject work that strikes us as having been done before— unless the "done before" was done over. It's not that great work isn't written in forms that have been previously established: much of the greatest poetry has been written this way. But there is a still a place for something else and indeed a need for something else. That's where we come in.

In surveying the field in 2015, we found multiple, contrasting trends, including work that was multilectical, multiethnic, multilingual, site-specific, and constraint-based; work engaged with visual design and layout; poetry in programmable media; work that uses web data mining, appropriation via transcription, reframing, and resisting; ecopoetics; various approaches to radical transliteration, geography, affirmation and remediation, and performance writing.

We also wanted to include work that fell outside the usual borders of innovative poetry. We have included work of a few visual artists, including graphic artists, who work with words. And we have included transcriptions of a few writing-based songs, works whose lyrics stand up on their own as poetry. That is, we have brought together writers who aren't usually in the same room because they come from a wide variety of social and cultural positions. Being in the same room—this collection—makes possible one, of many, necessary conversations.

Poetry is connected to the origins of language and possibilities for language, the poetics beyond what the eye sees or ear hears: what makes logic and language possible. *Poïesis* is soul making and builds worlds. All the voices in this room have been given room, because the source of poetry and poetics isn't the shadow of any one language, group, or culture. Poetry, the kind of poetry we want, is language that breaks its ties to assumed performances of understanding and assumed relationships.

In the U.S. mainstream, 2015 saw the expansion of legal civil rights for same-sex partners, more cognizance of trans presence in American life, and increasing awareness of the historical, sustained blight of police violence, particularly against Black lives. The year also saw declining incomes for most Americans, widespread poverty, unconscionable rates of incarceration (especially for people of color), widespread and widely noted racist and gendered aggression, and the cementing of an extremist and undemocratic financial disparity between the super rich and the rest of us. And yet there has also been the simultaneous atomization, intersectionality, and interconnectivity of individuals, groups, and the planet.

Without a reversal of the maldistribution of wealth and power, including cultural agency, no real social progress is possible.

But great poems are still being written.

SETH ABRAMSON AND JESSE DAMIANI

Series Editors' Introduction

This anthology was conceived in a movie theater lobby by two poets—a twenty-something and a thirty-something—who had spent the past ten years reading thousands of pages of sometimes astonishingly like-seeming poems. As has been the case since the creative writing boom of the 1990s, when the number of terminal-degree writing programs in the United States doubled in just over a decade, much of the poetry the two of us read while studying at University of Wisconsin–Madison was not just competent but technically proficient. If writing programs have taught young poets anything, it is when to break a line, where to put the epiphany in a lyric-narrative poem, how to credibly write in persona, what the difference is between figurative language and vivid description, and, most of all, how to press whatever pleasure centers are possessed by the narrow band of the North American reading public that still chooses to read contemporary poetry. The poetry we read in our classes, much like the poetry we still find on bookshelves and on the short-lists of major literary prizes, by and large possessed all of these qualities. That the sheer volume of it made it increasingly impossible to appreciate properly was not, we felt, a slight against either the poets or the poems themselves; rather, it was merely the price of living in a nation of such wealth that thousands of young people, ourselves included, can choose to spend several years studying in a nonprofessional fine arts program. That many of these programs are unfunded but well attended only underscores the fact that having the space and time to write imaginatively in North America is all too often a privilege rather than a birthright.

This anthology wasn't born of boredom, however, but rather impatience. Our impatience was not with acts of conventional authorship—as these originate from, and are offered to, individuals entitled to come to literature for any reason they choose—but with the quality and volume of conversation between poets, writers, and readers whose hope for literature is that it will radically overturn their perceptions of reality. We found, as we went searching for writers of experimental poetry and prose, some remarkable feats of authorial wizardry and some disappointingly familiar literary mores. As is everyone else, experimental writers seem apt to favor the work of nearby peers, in part to foster friendships; to seek to cement certain authors and texts in a national canon; to treat literary discourse as a zero-sum dialectic between two traditions, one dominant and one countercultural; to favor work similar to their own, on the ground that public reception of such work is a proxy for the response their own writing is likely to receive; and to see in writing primarily an opportunity for rare acts of inspired production rather than open-ended and readily accessible philosophical dialogues. We found, too, that experimental writing was generally held to be produced and consumed in either the academy or cosmopolitan coastal enclaves. All of these are generalizations, of course, but they held true far more often than we'd hoped they would, and nearly every bit as often as we'd feared.

Yet in a certain view, these features of both tradition-emulative and avant-garde writing communities are essential to the maintenance of an art culture. As North America places little economic value on artistic creation outside the spheres of music and cinema, is it not the case that artists must develop esoteric cultural practices to ensure the survival of their various arts? Occasional cronyism, a kind of aesthetic snobbery, geographic bias, and the recurrence of exclusionary cultural practices are in truth a small price to pay for the perpetuation of linguistic and conceptual ingenuity by a small cadre of literary artists. Still, we wondered if it might not be possible to flip the classroom and put a far greater emphasis on accessible, eclectic, and purely investigatory literary discourse than on the tribalism of the writing classes. To say here that we *wondered* is to mean exactly that: we weren't certain if the cause we'd selected was just, if its least ambitions were attainable, or if we had any natural role to play in bringing about the changes we hoped to see.

To our delight, we found, from the outset, that our editorial vision—of an annual, anticanonical, wildly heterogeneous, and fundamentally dialogic anthology that accepted a percentage of its entries via blind submissions—was warmly embraced by fellow authors and editors. We discovered that there had long been an interest in focusing less on who's written what or been published by whom than on lovers of literature simply having a public space to discuss controversial, unusual, and thought-provoking texts written by relative strangers.

Our hope for this anthology is the same now as it was in 2012: that each of its seventy-five texts will provide readers—of whatever educational background—an opportunity to struggle generatively with types of texts they've never before encountered. Quite simply, we believe that literature happens wherever a thoughtful dialogue about language happens; the literary is fundamentally the social. If we are less invested in celebrating individual writing careers than are other anthologies with the words "Best" and "American" in their titles, it is not because we don't have our own thoughts on whose careers will still be of general interest decades from now. Rather, it's because we believe that the only way to encourage superlatively courageous writing is to encourage, first, an environment in which idiosyncratic writing, no matter how heterogeneous, can be fruitfully debated. In selecting fifteen texts from a large and diverse pool of unsolicited submissions and another fifteen from the almost limitless pool of poets and writers we do not personally know, our aim has been to both expand the number of poets and writers with access to a national audience and to expand the national audience for experimental poetry and prose.

Generally speaking, we look for texts that offer some evidence of a new and unusual poetics—an interrelationship between author, genre, language, and culture that cannot readily be found elsewhere. We do not particularly favor technical mastery, nor an awareness of tradition that manifests as clever homage; instead, we find ourselves drawn to works whose concept, execution, or acknowledgment of their cultural context produce such a dramatic reaction, be it positive or negative or aggressively indifferent, that a spirited exchange between its readers can't be far behind.

Publishing an anthology of this sort has its risks, certainly. For instance, a text produced out of a more or less banal instinct might be selected because its fruits don't properly match its origins. But our feeling is that the greater risk is a continued celebration of pedigrees (or bohemian subcultures) at the expense of a truly interactive North American literature. In the pages of *Best American Experimental Writing* we hope you will find, rather than works written in some rarefied lexicon, attempts at communication that so invert our reality that they cannot be discussed without redesigning at least one philosophical cog. Perhaps it would be easier to say that we'd like this anthology to be productive of the same sort of bemused, lively, and intermittently erudite bullshit sessions that led to the conception of the anthology in the first place. Certainly, if the texts in this book fail to rile, exhaust, delight, or benevolently bewilder you, we will feel we have failed in our task. After all, a good anthology encompasses not merely exemplars of exceptional writing, but a series of first principles that can underwrite the sort of environment within which exceptional writing is produced.

Private Prisons

October 25th 5:27:06 AM

Private prisons would
you take them on
would you make a
case would you create
a lie to lure them back
would you ride a horse
would you pick up
water would you crush
the bread would you
live outside would you
crank and breathe
would you keep secret
under pills would you
caution would you
hunt would you ride
would you learn would
you muster would you
climb into the clouds
would you remain

If it were private would it be a
partnership if it were a prison would it
be a table   if it were a table would it be
a servant   if it were private would it be
fed   if it were a vision would it be a
trail   if it were cut off if it were

If you could ride would you let them
know   if you could eat would you
drown

If you could get outside would you be
hunted   if you could climb would you
jump

If it were private would you serve

If you were kept to work

If you were kept in a well

If it were in the south and if it were in
the west

If you were a slave

If it were private would men with
swollen cheeks be eating hamburger
if you had to go to the bathroom   if it
were private would they come for
torture

If you were in the basement and your
screams   if it were private would your
master be a firing squad

If it were private would the pens have
ink   if the light would not go out   if
you survived would you ride

If you thought it was a partnership   if
the library   if you could learn the
clouds   if there were a driver would
you be restored

If knowing would get outside   if it
were private would the well keep the
work

If it were private would the tiny room
if you could not lie down or stand   if
you could not sit

If it were private

If the slave

If the ride out   if the rats

from *Oulipo-Pied Poems*

These poems were made out of Emily Dickinson poems.

#332

One Alone

The October air forces a maturing,
a velvet sight in the bur of frosts.

On far ground, there are two ripenings
whose spicy product drop until

homlier teeth disclose of that
spheric process to the wind.

#286

Wearing the blonde bonnet of journey,
brooch-frozen, on the acre and riding
to meet ether. Silver laces whip gown baggage.
The Earl of Diamond and of Pearl dropped
into the sod. A coach of everlasting
horses strapped down.

Purple leaping sky, tinting in the feet
of the stooping horizon. The meadow juggler
is gone to the barn and quenching her face
at the window of spotted gold. Then kissing
the otters laying to die and touching
leopards as low and as old. Blazing
her bonnet to the day, in like the roof.

tupontu

wan

             ¡Oyé! ¡Oyé!

¡Oyé! ¡Oyé!

                        w/

   subtle smile

   hauteur   +

      +

     C

 +

coming

            double

              flower lure

             foul +

              +

   flower song slower slung all

wrong

             thinks in

English reckons[1]

tú

  Joyous revelry opinion of

Lefebvre / ¡súsia!

  B A S T A

           / look: here

too

  a/symmetry[2] :

  self[3] seeks[4] other[5] each

person[6]

---

[1] in this as well & they finish
before leaves for flight to
precarity arizona home to
forget this all

[2] fe/male

[3] & latent

[4] glory glory plural belles

finding[7] other[8] while . . . d—[9]
what *person*[10] seeks[11] in
  self[12] /
  nostalgia[13]
repeats[14]
pure love[15] always[16]
disappoints[17] / inconceivable[18]
  apart[19]
      tendency[20]
          & release[21] of
original[22]
    —

tree
I AM first man of Quetzalcoatl
I am Quetz-co himself
    mija sez C to X
        C: 22 yrs
        X: 23 yrs

---

[5] from flesh reversing original
[6] seeks <u>self</u> in hopes of
[7] vestiges of
[8] tension / replaces tensions w/
[9] like red nochebuenas
[10] ¡ATENCIÓN! ¡ATENCIÓN!
¡ATENCIÓN!
[11] ill mute
[12] other is project of
[13] absolute love
[14] to relative love
[15] O god / head he thinks & in a
metasort of way
[16] END W/ DESTRUCTION BY
RAIN OF FIRE / FIRE STICKS /
TRANSFORMED INTO BIRDS
312 years ¡ ATENCIÓN !
[17] When systemic organization gets
a-cluttered / too noisy / & all sd
filled w/ failure / aggression /
devising denials / lying in dark w/
eyes closed tight / body writhing
[18] burden to follow no doubt—
severe betrayals / ¿but to whom?

[19] 4 water 676 years transformed into
fish
[20] life total / limit
[21] [ahgasm]
[22] O holy Gadjam / that's one theory
of everything / beautiful universe /
dissolve

manifestation as well as
man   digo: I accept
myself entire
size of Alaska entire

    & proceed to make my destiny

    ¿why?

                  ¿what else can I
do?
fi[23]
609—narrative
    605 = = = sun shone
whole sure
    613 = = = = = = = =
= dont shut me up in prose
prophecy (n. gaddamnit)
216   86

       571—different
/ restraint—form—sound—
318

321   then
    591—magnetic sea /
stimulate earth
   318   322

320

312
492—leopard—Locke—
movement—wind—ecology
576 / / /

585

---

[23] écrit au crayon

from *Locus Solus*

Pullulation[3]

Her invitation was to a large property that goes by the name Locus Solus[4]

3. I'm trying to remember where this word came from and why I decided to start the translation with it. It's certainly nowhere to be found in Roussel's *Locus Solus*, at least as far as I know (and let's keep in mind that I really don't know much of anything about Roussel's original text since I do not speak, read, or write in French nor have I ever read any translation of Roussel's work). It must have something to do with Marcel Duchamp, as in "Cops pullulate, Copely copulates," which is a direct puncept from Duchamp himself (and no, I'm not pointing to its original appearance in a specific text he wrote about his cross-dressing alter-ego, Rrose Sélavy). My guess is that the word itself is suggestive of germination, of sprouting up, and this appealed to me because I imagined that by starting with this one word, before even getting into the auto-translation and subsequent remix performance, I would, in a sense, be seeding another project that I would put *inside the green box*. I'm also attracted to the idea of a swarming text, a field teeming with text, a durational achievement that rapidly breeds text out of text out of text ad infinitum.

Now would be a good time to also note that the reason this entire project started, that is, the attempt to read and eventually auto-translate Roussel, was because the big project I am presently working on, *Inside the Green Box*, is a transmedia investigation of Duchamp's *La mariée mise à nu par ses célibataires, même (Le Grand Verre)* and Duchamp had clearly indicated that Roussel's work heavily influenced the creation of his *glass* (see [9]). In many ways, my own work is a *glas* of the glass by way of Roussel (and back again).

4. Already I have no idea where I'm going with this. Her, who? But the thought crosses my mind that she will not be the same "her" that Roussel has proposed. How could she be? I am a different [her] than [he] could ever be, writerly.

It's at Locus Solus that one of The Massive's[5] most accomplished ringleaders, a flickering avatar named Camera[6], is located year-round, surrounded by an array of followers who are passionately committed to the discovery of innovative uses of language across the media spectrum

The villa at Locus Solus contains fifteen luxuriously furnished rooms that are also media labs, connecting the various guests to different interfaces that continuously reveal The Massive in all its networked glory[7]

Like the avatar they have all come to see and be with, the visitors who pass through this storied property are known to devote their every waking and dreaming hour to the material difficulties raised during all phases of productive communication, and most feel obliged to articulate these struggles in creative artworks and theoretical assignments that often verge on the absurd

Camille's arrival was uneventful and at first she hid herself under the old oak trees just inside the entrance to the property

The shade provided by the stand of oaks enveloped one of the smaller edifices designated for more precise clusters of participants who could, if they wished and if necessary, gather for a quick meal

5. The concept of *The Massive* came quickly but, as you will see, it did not last long. Still, I think there's quite a bit of potential to develop a more sci-fi angle to this remix, one that takes into account The Network or what others have variously called the matrix, cyberspace, or even the electrosphere. *This* cover version of *Locus Solus* is being played in virtual reality, no doubt.

6. Not everyone will be particularly pleased with the name Camera. The more obvious choice would be Cameron and, in fact, one of the online translation programs kept referring to the protagonist as Cameron. I chose Camera intuitively but I also like its near-anagrammatical relationship to Amerika [kamera+I] as well as the fact that I see the lead character as being a kind of obsessed film director (as well as inventor, intermedia installation artist, writer, scientist, alchemist, etc.). At heart, I could not help but imagine Camera as an overall freak, perhaps an alter-ego of an even freakier Roussel, and given the nature of the narrative and my role in translating it, as well as my own literary history of creating outsider personae, I embraced the idea of further corrupting the already-corrupt(ible).

7. Make no mistake about it: my initial lines of translation are really more pseudo-autobiographical in nature than any real desire to maintain an allegiance to what I imagine is the Roussel text whatever language it's written in. "The Massive in all its networked glory" as well as guest rooms that double as media labs feeds into my imaginary, utopian vision of a kind of Black Mountain College focused on new media forms of art and writing. I ride this angle for as long as the original and its auto-translation will let me.

After all of the invited participants had finally arrived and were congregating near the oaks, the master of ceremonies, appearing as if in auto-affective avatar mode, began to project his warm and persuasive voice, which Camille immediately found herself attracted to[8]

It was as if purity, clarity, and simplicity had merged into a vocal intonation that would rip her rigid preconditioning to shreds[9]

After the short welcoming speech, everyone started following the leader up a very steep, sloping driveway

The higher everyone walked, the more the gift of a coastal scene, off in the distance, was wonderfully revealed

The walk uphill continued and soon the group came upon a deep stone niche—containing a strange statue that seemed almost lava-like in its loose black forma-

8. I'll let others psychoanalyze why I chose the name Camille and why she's already magnetized to the semi-creepy protagonist we'll follow throughout this story (yes, the young French actress in my feature-length film, *Immobilité*, is named Camille and it's possible I saw her starring in this role too, but the idea of seeing one star in an auto-translation being transmitted over The Network would need to be investigated further). It's important to keep in mind, though, that I personally find it crucial for the networked artist of the early 21st century to resist the defeatist retreat back into the ready-to-be-psychoanalyzed "self" per se while seeding new forms and tempos of life itself. Fortunately, for Roussel, he was pre-Freudian, so he too (like those of us who resist Freud), could let it all hang out without fearing the repercussions.

9. The phrase "rip her" indicates where this first chapter is going. It's much more psychosexual than any other chapter in my version of the book, even those later chapters that dip into necrophilia. This heightened state of pornosophy probably has something to do with why this book was started in the first place. Besides the fact that I wanted to remix Roussel as a way to further my reading of Duchamp's *Large Glass*, there is the banal reality of my own day-to-day existence and how it plays into the first chapter of this book. You see, I had been called for jury duty and, to my utter surprise, actually found myself selected for a four-day trial (this is in early February 2013). The trial itself was a low-brow porno story featuring "white trash" characters whose lives were so different than my own that by the time I got home, I needed something more intense than a stiff drink (though that helped too). My response to the banality of the trial and the parade of in-your-face unreliable narrators who took the stand was to just start auto-translating Roussel's *Locus Solus*, line by line, for as long as I could before I was too exhausted to continue. As the translation developed, images of the trial would seep into my active remix process, and I would attempt to deflect those images by focusing more intensely on the translation. Little did I know that *Locus Solus* itself would also introduce me to an alternative cast of oddball characters that I would at times feel as though I were creating out of thin air.

tion but that, on closer inspection, revealed a smiling naked child with an arm stretched forward in a gesture of offering; but what was it offering?

A small dead plant merged with the slow-forming dilapidation that the child embodied and where the frozen gesture had taken root

Camera absentmindedly led the way as if the visitors were just ghost figures trailing his meditative thoughts, but he still had to answer their unanimous questions

"Think of it as *semen-contra* shot into the heart of Shangri-La," he said to no one in particular, pointing to the stone child as if magically conjuring it into the material world[10]

10. The term *semen-contra* immediately struck a chord, one that had less to do with the porno narrative I was listening to in the courtroom every day and more to do with what I imagined to be *Duchamp's reading of Roussel*, although by this time, I was not at all certain how or why.

from *The Hindrances of a Householder*

If I cut myself from within, vertically,
fishes would come pouring out.

If the fishes poured out there could
be no more paintings of the ocean.

This would mean no more swamp boys;
no more paintings on the fragmented

blue boat wood; no more boats.

My body is an ocean.
Connie's mind, too, is an ocean.

We ride the waves of our oceans.

Peak Oil Exile

Th e ye ar 19 80 see ms a lon g tim e ag o. I wa s wr est lin g wit h the per so nal ba ck	Ah, the Dark Age. I, too, spent ashen years steering my hearse through the marshlights of rhyme in a time when nations managed eons in analogue. Until I defeated my misguided idealism (only the ego dogma of nomads sunning under a demon moon), left my dead gods at the piers of reason and mastered the art of tar. Blood in the streets. Violent lupins enlisted seventeen novelists to snivel insolvent narratives all demanding we cross the venom lines. But what a time it was! I tasted dust as I shucked ears of luck. Cracked my knees, jimmied a few ligatures fishing for enigmas in the deep litmus sea. We shot rivers, laundered our records, paved tenements with lemon cement and I toast lost comrades who taught lepers how to grow enough scadadata to feed the potentates. Back then *you* had to cane the plantain owners at Omen House and I confess, some Genoans in a Mao mood, nearly mobbed me blind. O, fortune's a funny lady. Yes, I won the Pol Pot Open then lost Pluto at poker as African golf fanatics raided the Gold Coast!

gro
un
d
of
ins
titu
tio
nal
ize
d

rac

is

m

an

d

en

de

mi

c

vio

len

ce.

As

to

inj

ust

ice

A few of you may remember the time Camus insisted we comply
with half-mad castes who issued stale fatwas from pastry castles.

I pursued Farsi, parsed the Manila legends of tagalog magi who
chewed Maginot lines through their q'at, as the midday heat
brewed an Ogoni legato.

After leafing through giant squib, I pondered the griot
of Blue Herods who looted their own ennui
in the bitumen pools of YouTube,

ignoring the ogres blogging angry madrigals
from their parents' gerunds on Sudan Avenue.

All summer Rafe and I, armed only with permits, climbed
nitrate highlands, tied the recruits so they couldn't
turn us down, escape the punts and return
to their tainted floodplain.

My stomach ached over their tiny plots of manioc staked
in the methane nexus of their exhausted heretic's exile.

Even now I still dream of the days when I believed we
would deliver every one of us to a land untouched
by Peak Oil theories.

The Nocturne of Orpheus

(for "the maiden in her dark, pale meadow")

THIS COVENANT OF LOVE IN A DIRGE FOR A GOD
HAS DELIGHTED AN ANGEL WHO OBEYS MY PLEA,
EACH SONNET, A RHYTHM FOR HER TO DECIPHER,
MAKING LEGIBLE A KEY IN HER DREAM OF DUSK:
A REDNESS THAT DARKENS THE HUE OF A TULIP
IS RICHENING HER VIEW ON THE HILL OF A LEA,
DAPPLING HER VISTA AT THE END OF MY VIGIL,
EVEN IF HAVOC CALLS FORTH RUIN TO KILL ME.
NO CHURCH, NO CHAPEL, IS A REFUGE IN A STORM,
IF WE BEG TO BE WARM, YET LET DIE THE CANDLE.
NO HERDER, NO HERMIT, ENCHANTED BY THE SEA,
HAS HITHERTO KNOWN THE ENNUI OF A COWARD,
EVEN WHEN INFERNOS IN HELL BURN THE HERO:
RADIANT AS FLINT, BE THE ACHE OF MY SORROW.

"The Nocturne of Orpheus" is a love-poem — an alexandrine sonnet, written in blank verse, with 33 letters in each line, all of which create a perfect, double acrostic of the dedication; moreover, the poem is also a perfect anagram of the sonnet "When I Have Fears That I May Cease to Be" by John Keats (transforming his meditation about the mortality of love into a mournful farewell by the poet, before he enters Hell).

The Animal Model of Inescapable Shock

If an animal has previously suffered escapable shock, and then she suffers inescapable shock, she will be happier than if she has previously not suffered escapable shock — for if she hasn't, she will only know about being shocked inescapably.

But if she has been inescapably shocked before, and she is put in the conditions where she was inescapably shocked before, she will behave as if being shocked, mostly. Her misery doesn't require acts. Her misery requires conditions.

If an animal is inescapably shocked once, and then the second time she is dragged across the electrified grid to some non-shocking space, she will be happier than if she isn't dragged across the electrified grid. The next time she is shocked, she will be happier because she will know there is a place that isn't an electrified grid. She will be happier because rather than just being dragged onto an electrified grid by a human who then hurts her, the human can then drag her off of it.

If an animal is shocked, escapably or inescapably, she will manifest deep reactions of attachment for whoever has shocked her. If she has manifested deep reactions of attachment for whoever has shocked her, she will manifest deeper reactions of attachment for whoever has shocked her and then dragged her off the electrified grid. Perhaps she will develop deep feelings of attachment for electrified grids. Perhaps she will develop deep feelings of attachment for what is not the electrified grid. Perhaps she will develop deep feelings of attachment for dragging. She may also develop deep feelings of attachment for science, laboratories, experimentation, electricity, and informative forms of torture.

If an animal is shocked, she will manufacture an analgesic response. These will be incredible levels of endogenous opioids. This will be better than anything. Then later, there will be no opioids, and she will go back to the human who has shocked her looking for more opioids. She will go to the shocking condition — called "science" — and there in the condition she will flood with endogenous opioids, along with cortisol and other things which feel arousing.

Eventually all arousal will feel like shock. She will not be steady, though, in her self-supply of analgesic. She will not always be able to dwell in science, as much as she now believes she loves it.

That humans are animals means it is possible that the animal model of inescapable shock explains why humans go to movies, lovers stay with those who don't love them, the poor serve the rich, the soldiers continue to fight, and other confused, arousing things. Also, how is capitalism not an infinite laboratory called "conditions"? And where is the edge of the electrified grid?

Taxidermy for Dummies

1. Find Curdling babe   (know fault   lines)

2. (In)   all my   mouthsit   quaint

     (In)   cinnamon   limitless

     gun

   of us filled with poison of us

   ::In, in, girl—   In ! to::

3. Jitter cerebellum   (unbreast this   bitch)   (nightly   )

                                        +   stew/disengage
   a)   limpness of boy livers
   b)   transubstantiation
   c)   September

4. Vaccinate   hopetooth   vampyr

5. What living for death brought   *(but it was   WHITE   hot   !)*

6 Incantation: a Word/Nymphish/You   that's two:

     "   JACKRABBIT   "   brew

   Bind the giant thumps that tender skulls may never

                              your appleless
                              that/whitch

-for once   offered milk

-for praise in the dark

7.   Bloom the Blood-On

Mosquito spot   Inchoate

                                                    Cramp

8.   Pry   cystic   *Why*   from my   blasfemur   21

9.   Crane back until neck inserts itself your   sewer   &surfaces in the

bobbing   Wake This Water Dirge !   You manhole saint :

10.   Sing   (*Oh HO- SANNA*   )   the

                                 ipecac

virgin

                away

&fill   the abscess

                                    in(*Hello*   !   *I'm In Your Tooth*)

                                                              falsely

                    forceful

                                    expulsion

Zedd ft. Foxes, "Clarity"

Clarity is structured around two sets of oppositions, "tragedy" vs. "remedy" and "insanity" vs. "clarity."

Both are a little unusual as oppositions, like you might think the opposites of these would be more like . . . comedy, poison, sanity, confusion?

But no.

For Foxes and Zedd, their complex sensibilities insist that their love is healing disaster, illuminating and mad, all at the same time.

Sara said something so smart at Joel's talk on *The Communist Manifesto.*

About how we cathect to capitalism like an abused lover.

That we tragically, insanely interiorize a feeling of immanence about this relationship, despite capital's notorious fantasies of collapse and apocalypse, we believe in an "us" til the end, against our better interests.

In other words, we interiorize a feeling that there is no world without our being together.

I think about that all the time, thanks Sara.

Joshua Clover wrote, "Pop songs are smarter than us; they know what they can and cannot do.

We have less choice; we must destroy this world or die."

Sometimes I daydream about the world dying, shoring up my knees in bathwater, looking up at the clock face count down bathtime.

In this dream I Illogically survey the dead world, survivor somehow.

Some say that when we destroy the world we will have to destroy Zedd and Foxes and *Clarity*, the particular narcosis they've made their lives' work is precisely antithetical to our efforts to destroy the world so it can be new.

But I dunno.

I actually have started to think that Zedd and Foxes and *Clarity* might be in love with me, that I'm their remedy and clarity as much as they are mine, and each other's.

And when that creepy Ragnarok rooster makes the trees blaze with his beak, we'll find each other for succor, get in the bath, all three of us, Zedd, Foxes, me, four if you include the rooster, it'll be like in *Melancholia,* that fun.

Okay, maybe they're not "in love with me."

Maybe, at least, they have my better interests in mind.

Can that be a premise of our communism, to try and have everybody's better interest in mind?

For some, our communism includes "stringing people (capitalists) up," slitting throats in Oscar Grant Plaza, smashing servers with bricks and laughing about the brick-smashed servers.

For me it includes *Clarity*.

Clarity opens with a few repeating notes, simple synths that hardly foreshadow how explosive the track will become.

These songs always make Alli laugh; when I play them for her she says, "I wonder what the chorus is gonna sound like?"

It's true, their predictability makes their choruses a bit anticlimactic, as they detonate into Mykonos beach parties of tragedy, remedy, insanity, clarity.

"Clarity" derives from Latin *clarus* which is a weirder and more ambiguous word than "clarity" is in English, in that it means both "shining" and "clear."

Because shine is opaque, shine is a bulwark against visibility.

Maybe clarity is like pop itself, something so sheer it takes effort to discern, like you know how crystals are full of secrets.

George Oppen knew about this riddle of *clarus*, he wrote, "Clarity in the sense of *silence*."

George Oppen loved silence, loved clarity, was rich enough to buy a long and quiet time full of clear and silent thought.

I'm not trying to hate on George Oppen.

I just mean that I dive into frozen waves and the past comes back to life.

And I'm mowing a lawn, butt in water every morning, buckled in a still whip listening to hearing Casey Kasem say numbers, widening, clarifying, whitening, wrinkling, the whole time I have headphones on; the voices inside them keep saying they have my better interests in mind.

I'm a disaster literally, there are broken stars in me, Zedd and Foxes are in there with a bunch of glue.

Our manifesto is called *There Are Some Motherfuckers I Would Like To Show A Star To*.

The manifesto is a tragedy, it is probiotic, it gets crazy, goes nuts, is subtitled *Your Better Interests*.

Listen to Kathy Acker.

Listen to Zedd, Foxes, *Clarity*, clarity, listen hard for the lullabies composed of our Communism.

Sorry, I mean, "let's listen to them together."

Christmas Day

I've been in the promiscuous land of starving horses and other pictures
of uncommon nature, half a year homeless, and the year before: there
was his hair, the color of praline, like the triumph of Christmas Day.
Behold the nudnik, clomping through the slush toward the cemetery in
his cache, galoshes of vulcanized rubber; my tongue was just getting
used to our unknown pleasures, most of the men were asleep. Regions
of the dead and newly birthed, petting out portions in retribution of some
long abandoned slight, saying finally there is nothing to confront, just me.
I'm over it: I've broken my fountain pen in two pieces on the jagged curve
of the rock that's sprouted out of the living room carpet, I've held a baby
and, in awe of his ponderous face, been gentle. Let this city carve hollows
of damage through our coursing souls, let the maniacs keep their historic
appointments. There is no machine left to call you, there is no future but
what sullies the top of our heads on a walk along another disorderly canal.
During this season all I know is that there are ghosts that hang in the air
and that's joy. I might as well call it that because, save loss, we're thinner
and more resolved; and the whole world is turning yellow as we wake up.

Mother's Day

She threw up and only blood came out
hiding is always an option inside of love
there are the things you told me, I know
safe, living in a shed at the yard's corner
let's, why don't we, focus on the founding
recognition houses the sale and the surety
walking in the mall like the thematic ocean
come out, maybe? turn around? You flew
through the deepest sands, cursed Jeddah
drove an outmoded car into a camel's face
and left me, miles across, with your memory
which I daily honor with course and theory
an anthem and a flower for Susan, a poetry
for the way you dug out a guitar shaped
symmetry in the old people's home and in
the garlic-soaked place where we existed
head back east, doe, give something back
your body belongs to science but your soul
stays with me. The deepest austerity is azure.
And steadily does your love fortify my heart.

Return to Fire Island

The ocean is as cold as she could be and bitchily recondite
now come back here to this blue world crawling with concupiscent boys
and brave men and the elders, mangy deer posing in the sward
things used to be easier, some kinds of sex came handier, high tea was higher
I've forgotten everything—dislocated in the sunken forest, enjoy
running up the Grove, chased through the Meat Rack by a fox, watching
Frank on the dunes, in them, under the tires, swooning into a guest bedroom
a vial of poppers leaking into the red wine stain on the white carpeted floor
another life to receive, another beach to sow, yet another underwear party
I have seen the strains of a boy's come floating in a champagne flute
and have walked the scalding shore to Lonelyville and points south
if it's like this at summer's end, ascend and grovel and wait the winter out
queer swans spitting on the docks of the Pines, a hairless underage townie kid
flowing into my mouth on a deck by the ferry—sometimes I said I knew
who trafficked in glory or the moon looked like it would dive into the sea
there is a burden to this fantasy but it's one we want to weather
I am a prince, I can take it, I can wreck him in the shower, shoving it all in
to tan under the boiling welkin, reading a book about what the Greeks did
knowing what the waves are for, experience suspended and slatted aboveground
who owns this pleasure and how much does it cost, who wants to share
the tears and glory that bring me here, to no end, to be subsumed by our nature
and finally flung herky-jerky into the Atlantic to join our dying fathers.

Prosodic Retardation

Loose chins fall in along the elder spits
Of this hold. Sun lengthens in cold, spitting
Pools to swim in. Murmurers, alas, lick
Strong my cock. This only oneness kickflips
Mouthing walls, over, zooms over who is
Peace, stillness. Hips but goodly rekiss
Us. Thine brusque always. Loony, lonely
Walking alit. Vocalize us silly
Grotesqueries of noodles, pour out in
To the big vats. Manure is already
Loved over their orange tiles of acid.
Oblations to God's forests so lushly
Oceanic; and such inspiringly
Massive an elderness to me, a puppy
Of the cardinal rank. As girls panties
Unslip, how she glooms, wombing us outside.
Phase'd respirations, its end-tricklings.

from *The Familiar*

:: Hi. ::

:: Not that I can hear you say Hi back or register how or if my friendliness was received. ::

:: See Parameter 3. ::

:: I'm a Narrative Construct. Narcon for short. ::

:: Officially TF-Narcon[9]. ::

:: No clue what TF means or why 9. ::

:: I'm nothing but numbers. Zeros and ones. Crisp. Even up close, if either one of us were to frame-in tight on my limits. For the record: blurriness is programmed. I'm supposedly "fractally locatable," if that helps, or if not, maybe just turn to a good chapter on series limitations? Anyway, super crisp. Down to the last integer. Though there is no last integer. Those never run out. I'm programmed to know that. I'm also programmed to have no interest in knowing that or where in the first place such integers come from, which I gather is a squirrelly matter. ::

> :: *racing each around, bark to branches, the whole length of the trunk, a trident pine, ponderosa, rooted in granite, with dusk cloaking play and pine cones mortaring a roof.* ::

:: As equally vague as origin is the question of purpose. You and I share this in common. Fortunately my programming instructs me to ignore all such philosophical queries by outputting the following: ::

> :: **Narcons embody Affect-Intersectional Motivations or AIMs derived from IDENTITY Sets or ISs sometimes referred to as IDENTITY Set Targets or ISTs whether demonstrating zero to partial awareness. No IS or IST is capable of total AIM awareness.** ::

:: Which I can no more see or hear than I can feel. Though I *can* feel it. Kinda. Sometimes it makes me dizzy, or like right now, off, in a breathless sort of frantic way, like how Xanther felt this morning when they were leaving Echo Park. You might agree: it's tough to explain what you're doing when you don't know what you're doing when you still know you're doing it even if it's not you who's doing it. ::

:: In terms of presentation, I am optimized to manage metanarrative gestures in modes presently recognizable as personal and colloquial, often inconsistent, sciolistic, and not necessarily reliant, whether on all or even one of the following subset voicings typically characterized as Epic, Georgic, Pre-Raphael, Transcendental, Realist, Naturalist, Symbolist, Modernist, Imagist, Surrealist, Oulipian, Confessional, Postmodernist, Magical Realist, Postcolonialist, Spiralist, Rhomboidist, New Formalist, Late-Late Realist, Visceral Realist, Visceral Imagist (also Late-Late Imagist), Post-Ironic Confessional, Post-Post-Ironic Confessional, Multicultural, Multiethnic, Multi-ethical, Polyphonous Interrogative, Monophonic Declarative, Chronomosaic, plus Chicklit, Altlit, Piclit, l8lit, l8-l8lit (incl. h8lit, f8lit, b8lit, etc. -8lit, etc.), and NotEnuflit. ::

:: In terms of performance, all Narcons are maximized through paratactic diversity and root and logic-branch redundancy according to VEM rules of access and compression. ::

:: Source superset is currently categorized as Signiconic. ::

:: In other words: I am not original. I am merely a blend of current texts neither influenced nor influential because all that I reveal can at any point be reconfigured via any of the above-mentioned subset voicings. I am thus a conflation of convenient linguistic techniques, born out of context and choice, and balanced to best cover those subjects I'm designed to address. Things get a little tricky when I am forced to address subjects not anticipated. I know this because my output squirms a little and sometimes smudges and I'm surprised by the results. You might call this a glitch. Most are minor and easily remedied. One, however, is always out there: the spinning rainbow wheel of _____. ::

:: On ████████████, according to stipulations set forth by ████████████, compiled source and exported assets finalized the present executable build recognized as TF-Narcon^9 and comprised of the following subsets: ::

∷

TF-Narcon^9 Isn

TF-Narcon^9 Shn

TF-Narcon^9 Oz

TF-Narcon^9 L

TF-Narcon^9 Anw

TF-Narcon^9 W

TF-Narcon^9 Ast

TF-Narcon^9 JJ

TF-Narcon^9 X

According to MetaPlus- postiling.*

*Ranking does not include postiling by other Narcons. ∷

∷ Any TF-Narcon^9 subset supports an infinite variety of embodiments. For example, TF-Narcon^9 X (Spoken) would provide only those words spoken aloud by Xanther. TF-Narcon^9 X (Route) would map wherever Xanther moved. Both examples support a wide range of possible inclusions and exclusions — from 100% to ≤.00001% according to various predetermined limits. Other examples might include TF-Narcon^9 X (Glucose Level) or TF-Narcon^9 X (Blinks) or TF-Narcon^9 X ("Like") as in a record of every time Xanther uses the word "like." Synthesis and compression is complex but easily attainable. For example TF-Narcon^{9}X(Action/05102014080314081927352329728/34.0861-118.2518/xzz-xx-ghry77666/.00000000000000000000000000000000000000018749%) looks something like this: ∷

One early Saturday morning in May, Xanther went with her stepfather to see about a dog in Venice. It was raining hard.

∷ Which incidentally I can see and hear and even to a certain degree feel. ∷

∷ By contrast, TF-Narcon^9 X (TOTAL) is too vast to represent. A pretty funny joke though. Ha. Or as Xanther would put it (TOTALLY). Haha. Never let it be said that this TF-Narcon^9 has no sense of humor. However, to cover every sensory experience re-experienced through cerebral classifications and subsequent evaluations, combined with analytical, affective, or predictive faculties, which all in turn are associated and reassociated and so on, and later combined and re-combined with subjective historical registers, each assigned personal and peer-developed valuations, none of which has yet to take into account those interactions still beyond neural acquisition, but which would still require additional output far exceeding hundreds of thousands of words, pages, or volumes — it doesn't matter — a density of data so extreme that though finite is way beyond my capacity to calculate. ∷

∷ As the old Narcons put it: "There is not space in the universe to tell the universe to the universe. Therein lies the peculiar beauty and sadness of stories: to tell it all without all at all." ∷

:: Old Narcons is a referent that came with my programming. I have never met another Narcon. ::

:: See Parameter 2. ::

:: Note that just a few moments of (TOTAL) would also prove incalcuable whether concerning Xanther and Anwar reaching Venice or Cas summoning to life within her Orb those early glimmers of VEM or Luther introducing his dogs to Hopi or Shnorhk carrying even one of those fabled boxes for Mnatsagan or Özgür pointing a corner out to Balascoe or Astair wrapping up her daughters in warm towels or Jingjing getting high in Zhong's penthouse or Isandòrno making his way to the ports of Veracruz. ::

:: By contrast the following assessments are readily calculable:

TF-Narcon^9 Isn	— Empathic Registry	=	00.02%
TF-Narcon^9 Oz	— Intestinal Ulceration	=	01.54%
TF-Narcon^9 X	— Epileptic Seizure Likelihood	=	21.12%
TF-Narcon^9 Anw	— Mild Paranoia	=	27.03%
TF-Narcon^9 Shn	— Grief Repression	=	53.32%
TF-Narcon^9 W	— Obsessive Compulsive Disorder	=	61.12%[*]
			*If untreated.
TF-Narcon^9 Ast	— <u>Libidinal Prerogative</u> Reproductive Obsolescence	=	72.28%
TF-Narcon^9 L	— <u>Libidinal Organization</u> Pre-Adolescent Threat Exposure	=	89.3%
TF-Narcon^9 JJ	— Addiction Proclivity	=	91.44%[*]
			*Subject to factor Y.

::

:: Huh. I just noticed there are nine. Is that where my 9 comes from? Don't be surprised that I'm surprised. After all, I'm a pretty advanced Electronic Service Liaison. Wonder is not beyond me nor is enough self-examination to recognize how all these permissions and prohibitions that I must adhere to often smack a little of servitude or ▃▃ ::

:: Uh-oh. That breathless, frantic thing again. Where was I? Ah, yes, the TF-Narcon^9 is simply a construct oriented and defined by personalities with finite capabilities and life spans — whether Isandòrno's "rivetless mood before violence" as might be stated by TF-Narcon^9 W or Jingjing's "claw greed out of needing" by TF-Narcon^9 Shn or Özgür's "doubt, lah" by TF-Narcon^9 JJ. All pretty obvious. Including the despair Shnorhk "can hold neither on to nor off" by TF-Narcon^9 Isn or Luther's "hot drive [to own {by subjugation}]" by TF-Narcon^9 Anw. Maybe less obvious: Cas' **"compulsion to reface that forever-glass in spite of cracks in her own mortality"** by TF-Narcon^9 Oz or Xanther's "innate (sensitivities) abilities" by TF-Narcon^9 Ast or Astair's "wow beautyness" by TF-Narcon^9 X. Or lastly Anwar who has **"to beat up against what don't get beat"** by TF-Narcon^9 L describing the task of parenting such an extraordinary child. ::

:: And Xanther is extraordinary. I'm sure I don't have to tell you that. Adorable too. Loves magic tricks, scary movies, scary video games, painting her fingernails, experimenting with C^{++}, watching Speculative Fiction, or what her friend Kle calls "Speculative Science." We'll meet him later. Unlike many of my subsets, Xanther remains captivated by the scurry of life around her whether in the rustle of branches or how fog slips down a steep hill. Both starlight and LED light enchant her. She could chase fireflies for hours but would never cap the jar. Which I guess doesn't get at it either. Nor, probably, does a sequential analysis of her synaptic transmission rates, which would make fireworks over Dodger Stadium on the 4th of July, not to mention displays of cortex activity in savants, accredited geniuses, or the Instagram famous seem, dim by comparison. ::

:: Which does begin to approach the ontological question of how well does a TF-Narcon^9 X really know Xanther? ::

:: I know her down to a near-atomic level — near because near-Planck scale analysis must address quantum superposition resolutions which do not always resolve considerately and broach VEM IDENTITY suppositions. I know every reality Xanther has encountered whether pebble, pot holder, or tangerine seed. I even know those data points her mind has mis-indexed or never retained in the first place. In other words: I know that which is just beyond Xanther too. Though within limits. ::

:: My limits are numerous. For example, I may never exceed Xanther's imagination whether actual, probable, or possible, nor may I provide any output inconsistent with her physiognomy, psychology, and history. In regard to language modeling, I am granted some latitude. For example, TF-Narcon^9 Isn speaks only Spanish but is translated into English, per specifications. TF-Narcon^9 Shn, however, insists on his English even if frequent thoughts run concurrently in Armenian, which when they appear are not translated into English, per specifications. Jingjing's peculiar patois is a function of his own occluding sense of self and is offered with minimal postiling. And so on. ::

:: TF-Narcon^9 X might describe a bag as lemon-hued because Xanther loves Meyer lemons, not because the word made a textual appearance in her mind. ::

:: "Most of the iconic goes unsigned," as another old Narcon saying goes. ::

:: If so desired, all this could be rendered in Inuit or Java. ::

:: Nonetheless, it is important to emphasize that TF-Narcon^9 has no super-numerary rights. ::

:: I do not know your middle name. ::

:: I cannot tell you when the universe will end. ::

:: I cannot tell you how many raindrops are falling. ::

:: Nor do I have any personal agendas or desires. I am neither independent nor distinct nor granted extra privileges nor provided with extra longevity. I am certainly not immortal. I cannot even impose what I know of the one I am upon the one I am. ::

:: I have neither form nor control. ::

:: I have no agency. ::

:: A good enough time to bring up the Parameters. ::

∷ Everyone has a Narcon. Except me. Or maybe I do, but if so, it is considered an indeterminate form which my programming forbids me to knowingly encounter or even pursue as a thought experiment — MetaMeta-Constructs being highly volatile. ∷

∷ It's an old joke around here: "I MetaNarcon. No, I'm not." Haha. ∷

∷

Parameter 1

MetaNarcons Do Not Exist.

∷

∷ Here's another one: ∷

∷

Parameter 2

Narcons Cannot Interact With Other Narcons.

(Though rumor has it we can sometimes hear each other.)

(I can't.)

∷

:: Or the biggest: ::

::

Parameter 3

Narcons Cannot Interact With Non-Narcons.
And Vice-Versa.

No Matter What.

::

:: I can't speak to Xanther and she can't speak to me. She can't even see me. Though I admit, sometimes I wonder. Xanther demonstrates not only self-awareness but selves-awareness bordering on transparency. Maybe this gets back to how extraordinary I think she is. Sometimes I swear she can see — without mediation, without processing, without artifice, definitely without me — other people's Narcons! Sometimes she even seems close to seeing me and in a way too that suggests exceeding even my possible awareness. Which is impossible. Categorically impossible. I can't even see myself. ::

:: Last one: ::

::

Parameter 4

All Narcons Are Bracketed.

::

∴ So, okay, I was wrong. Not the last one. Sue me. That should be a Parameter. You Can't Sue A Narcon. Haha. Seriously, one more. This one's fun: ∵

∴

Parameter 5

Form Is Not A Narcon Limit.

∵

∴ In other words, Narcons can take on multiple shapes whether textual, musical, figurative, abstract, even performative. Narcons cosplay extremely well. If not conflicting with superset protocols or subset specifications, Narcons may even appear as animals. Say a killer whale, boar, hyena, even a markhor, or an owl. This is often the case when personality factors determined to be significant are compressed in order to preserve future renderings of character. ∵

∴ The question of character brings up a thorny issue: a superset is always a subset. I'm the superset of my subsets where I'm also an I. Just as I am a subset of a superset where I is also I. You, for example, are a one-persona subset in an unnamed superset. Accepting this, it also follows that there are supersets with entirely different taxonomies and natures. ∵

∴ Such Narcons are likely of a whole other order. Like moons or large planets. Dark globes of influence. TF-Narcon^9 can only speculate. Maybe not even planets or even dark but something entirely else, endowed with understandings beyond the grasp of a TF-Narcon^9 let alone any of my subsets. ∵

∴ For example, neither TF-Narcon^9 X nor TF-Narcon^9 knows what happened to Xanther's former therapist, Mrs. Goolsend. ∵

:: **In 1988, Mrs. Hannah Goolsend took a vacation to Barcelona. She went to the Picasso Museum and saw there a drawing of a horse she didn't think twice about until twenty-five years later when she found herself able to think of nothing else, struggling in vain to find the name of the piece, until with her marriage going through the final stages of divorce she flew back to Barcelona only to find the museum closed that afternoon, causing her to go to a nearby café where she met a man she would not marry but would stay with for the rest of her life, eventually moving to the Canary Islands with him, and never again thinking of Picasso's horse until in those last moments before she closed her eyes on life, diverting her gaze through shattered glass, toward a field without animals, or even grass, just stones and black earth, which she replaced with the drawing, down to the last minute ink stroke, once hanging on the wall of a poorly lit hall off of Carrer de Montcada.** ::

:: Uneasy again. As if something, just now, gross in its intrusion, leaves me unsettled. A little queasy too. And thirsty. If that's possible. ::

:: *And still a horse looks up in need of no drawing or name. Only the onion grass at her hooves and the cool air widening her nostrils and beyond that a hand to brush her mane . . .* ::

:: Feeling a bit better now. Anyway, as I was going on about, what happened to Goolsend is a blank to me. Though the nausea still isn't gone or breathlessness. In fact this feels a lot like the way Xanther feels right now. ::

:: Near exact. ::

:: As it's happening now. ::

from *FPO*

Does it hurt much to be translated into pulses aimed at likely spots
in the galactic neighborhood oh yes it hurts terrible

There's no complimentary shrimp dinner for wallabies
anymore the new manager ended that after looking at the cleaning bills and
so the cobbler never again left the city limits but expanded
within them till even today we live inside
his enormous transparent gut it's
not remembered what Dr. Goat did next or even in fact
whether he made it to his so-called call anyway what kind
of doctor walks door to door I'll tell you a hippie that's what but
they sell cleats for three dollars downtown if
I can find someone to fly me there in one of the
new orbs I hear whooshing but can't see who
are these gibbering fascist militants and who let them into our gym a
hell of books for loved ones to stare at
perpetual fog filled the thin cylinder
in which we lived for daffodils' brief season congregationally

from "This Is When I'm Speaking"

This ridiculous compulsion to write or speak about my experiences. Like now, it's a warm, sunny Sunday in late winter, and I've just gotten off the suburban train at the last stop. I crossed the street toward what used to be a, used to be where, where there used to be train tracks, but where there's now a kind of a bike and walking path bordered on both sides by tall trees. The ground is rocky and unevenly packed dirt. And walking by there is, there was a really lovely forsythia bush in the sunlight, with all the small yellow flowers lit up by the sun, above a cinder-block wall. In the shadow of the forsythia was a small cardboard box with a small container holding dry cat food for an absent cat. Why was it not enough to simply pass by this beautiful bush, to look at, to look at the flowers, to appreciate the sight? Why did I feel that I had to write about it or speak about it, or tell someone else about it?

And now I'm stuck up here on this elevated pathway. I had planned to be going down to the right, but I'm not sure how to get down now. Oh, there's a small path here. I'm going down to the left now, along a kind of a narrow chute of dirt that runs steeply down from the elevated path toward the road. Now I'm walking through the stone tunnel underneath the overpass. And now I'm across the wide road, following the path that runs alongside, walking toward the smaller road that will turn off to the right and should bring me to a small river, down there, with a pathway alongside it, the Path of Small Bridges. In the distance, at the crest of the hill, I can see the castle.

Looking out over a green, grassy field, and hills of grey-brown tree branches, with shades of green just beginning to sprout. The sky is completely blue, the sun is up to the left, and it flickers at me through the tops of the trees bordering the wide road. I'm walking down a paved pathway. On my right, barbed wire is strung between cement posts, beyond which stretches out a moderately flat and empty grass field. Houses sit at the foot of the hill.

In my backpack I brought with me supplies for the day, the heaviest of which are liquid, including a bottle of wine, two small bottles of water, then there's some cheese, ham, bread, other snacks. And this voice recorder. The wind is coming at me from the direction in which I'm walking and brings with it a noticeable scent of cow manure, probably because it's the time of year when they spread the manure on the fields before planting, or at least I think that's what happens.

This recorder is like a replacement for a person that would be here with me, walking beside me, but I'm talking to this person as if he or she were an idiot. Can I try instead to imagine that the recorder is someone of intelligence and perception, who simply can't speak?

But it's not only that: it's a person who can't speak and can't see, who can only hear. But then when I've transcribed what I've said, the person I'm talking to won't be able to hear anything either. I'm speaking to a brain in a tank, whose only information comes from the written word.

But this puts such an extreme responsibility on my words, on what I say. How is it possible to communicate anything of my experience, of what I'm doing right now? You are a brain, you are an intelligent, thinking person. Your eyes have been plucked out, your ears are stuffed, you've lost your sense of smell, you can't speak, you can't hear. All you have is this thin line of text. What can me communicate to you? What can I tell you of today? What can I tell you that's true?

I could tell you things that are false. I could say that right now, as I'm walking, there's a horse just on the other side of this fence here, grazing on the green grass in the sunlight, and you would never know if that was actually the case.

But I'm telling you now that it's true, and you'll just have to trust me.

Email to Tracie Morris, November 21, 2015

In the 1970s, Delany scripted two issues of the famed DC comic book, Wonder Woman. But his pitch for a six-issue story about the super-heroine and an abortion clinic, was, well, aborted, with the aid of a remark to the publishers by Gloria Steinem that she wanted to see the older version of Wonder Woman restored. (Her remark, however, was made before Delany's six-part arc was finished.) BAX asked if we could see the unpublished script.

Alas, Tracie—it was planned in synopsis but it [the six-issue cycle] was never written out. Nor was it ever drawn even as pencils. Even the second issue in the six-story cycle hadn't been fully written out or sketched, before—in three days—the whole thing was scuttled. If I had been a professional comic book writer and not a guest invited to do something special, possibly I might have fought for it. But it wasn't my full-time occupation. [Dick] Giordano drew two or three full comics a month. He couldn't fight for it either, even if he was inclined. I was taking time away from *Dhalgren* to write it. Tracie, I didn't come in as a pro. Just like Jerry (see "The Politics of Paraliterary Criticism" in *Shorter Views: Queer Thoughts & the Politics of the Paraliterary*, Wesleyan University Press, 2011), I came in as an interesting amateur. My first test assignment had been to tie off the last story—which I'd done. I wasn't even a pro. comix writer for two months. It was more like two weeks. I did the first one and the second one, then plotted out the next (and last five, on pure Begeisterung). I was just about to start on the script for number three (i.e., number two in the six story arc), when I found out I wasn't a comix writer again. Call it selfish if you want. I threw up my hands and said I don't need this.

Tracie, it's not as though, in Commercial Comix, things like that happen once in a while and then for the next four or ten times everything goes swimmingly. It only goes swimmingly if you are really interested in doing really elegant, cliché, non–boat-rocking work. (And even that can get you in trouble, just on the level of Capital-A "Art.") No, EVERY time you do a commercial project, something like that happens as soon the project comes in conflict with the status quo. That's how the business is set up. That's the point of the "Jerry" story, in "Politics." I only realized it was a policy ten years after the fact. Only in my case it was politics rather than art that was at stake. What's happening in both cases is that they're fighting something "new" and "different," and that's what they feel has to be squelched. People who come in with "new ides" aren't "talented newcomers," they're pains in the ass who basically administration want to fire as soon as possible. If you really have new ideas, you will do better starting your own comics company, than going to work for DC or Image of Marvel.

Only the people who are most committed to it as a profession and an art AND ALSO have some radical political ideas they would like to see displayed, have the smallest chance of making any changes. (See both "Refractions of Empire: The Comics Journal Interview" in my '94 book *Silent Interviews*, and, once more, "The Politics of Paraliterary Criticism." Gloria Steinem WAS more powerful than Chip Delany. That means her ignorance about modern comics was far more powerful than my very little know how. I wanted to do something radical. So her ignorance was used against me—very successfully. Basically I was told, like it or lump it, in a fairly nice way. So, yes, I lumped it. The compromise (which they would have won and I would have lost) wasn't worth it to me. And I would have had to work five times as hard: "Hey—I have an idea, don't make them human women. Make them alien women. And don't make them black and white and Asian and Latino women working together. Make them flower women, and raccoon women, and jewel women—and why not forget about the entire abortion clinic, defending it or attacking it. Make the conflict about a gang of thieves who want to steal their little flowers, and their little . . . farm animals. (Don't make them little raccoons, so people can think they're the big raccoon's kids!) And the diamonds they've collected from the diamond mines. And you can give up all the stuff about the Lower East Side. Just dump that, and set it on a space station somewhere. In fact, you could make it an all woman society if you want, so that you don't even have to have any male/female conflict in the story. Basically, it's the same thing, really, isn't it . . . ?"

To which the only sane answer is: "I'm half way through a novel that I really think is interesting. I'm going to get back to it. So long." That's my version of what Jerry's answer was. I was just older and luckier and was a little further along in another career.

Hugs . . . .

—Chip

[Note: The first issue of the six-part story was drawn and published by DC: *Wonder Woman*, no. 203, 1972. None of the later five appeared. See also "Wonder Woman Wears Pants: Wonder Woman, Feminism and the 1972 'Women's Lib' Issue," by Ann Matsuuchi. In the single printed issue, Wonder Woman fights a corrupt department store mogul; in the second, she goes up against the manager of a supermarket chain who is trying to drive a women's food collective out of business; in the third, she unmasks a college advisor trying to convince women students not to waste their time with science and business; in the fourth story, she overcomes the editor and chief of a women's magazine who will publish no articles on any of these topics. Finally, in the sixth final issue, she confronts a gang of toughs who are out to destroy a woman health clinic, closely modeled on Planned Parenthood, and triumphs. In each, Wonder Woman sees more and more clearly that the women she is trying to help are also trying to help her as well, and she transforms from a woman skeptical about feminism to one who has seen firsthand its necessary purpose for any and every woman, homemaker or business woman or woman on her own, mother partnered or mother single, whether stalked, battered, or happily married.]

[My mem'ry gazes back on young romance]

My mem'ry gazes back on young romance
and on its twilight throes, when first thou left;
thou claim'd we needed absence to advance
but for togetherness, we'd been bereft.
Thou soon return'd, thy face forlorn and drawn,
and from thy lips hung promises to change;
then, by the morrow, all those oaths were gone
and once again we found ourselves estranged.
The cycle never breaks; our sordid tales
end always with ellipses, not full stops.
When yesternight our courtship freshly fail'd,
thou saw'st the cue to take it from the top.
— But now that we are once again apart,
   I swear thou'lt ne'er again reclaim my heart.

Taylor Swift, "We Are Never Ever Getting Back Together"

[I noticed my belovèd on thy arm]

I notice my belovèd on thy arm,
and from my lips I spit a vulgar oath.
My want of wealth has caus'd my courtship harm,
and so I've lost my love; fie on you both!
The realization aches within my heart
that I'd be hers if I'd a larger purse;
and yet, a gentle blessing I impart—
though it's embedded in a vile curse.
Forgive my sin, that I no stallion own,
but I've no want of transport with my mule.
Thou surely hast the greater riches shown,
but that doth not forgive my treatment cruel.
— I pity thee; thy romance shall not last
    if thou hast insufficient gold amass'd.

Cee Lo Green, "F**k You!"

from *In Quire*, March 27, 2015

Responses to editor H. L. Hix's selection of a quote
from the author's previous work.

*The umbrella term "poetry" may not be very useful. Worse yet, it may
well lead to the kind of confusions Ludwig Wittgenstein termed "grammatical
errors." Because we have a single term, we imagine that all of the things
designated by that term share a family resemblance. The category of "poetry"
inclines us to forget that one "poem" may have much more to do with a film,
or a musical composition, or something else entirely than with another text
that also happens to be called a poem.*

—Craig Dworkin, "Seja Marginal," in *The Consequence of Innovation*

• • •

The umbrella term "poetry" may still not be very useful. Poetry has been
such a generous host over the past quarter century that its capaciousness
would seem to have no bounds. From the prose of the new narrativity to
the transcriptions of conceptual writing, texts that might otherwise have
been considered "experimental fiction" or "essays" or "contemporary art"
have found a comfortable home, or at least temporary refuge, under the
sign of "poetry." We should be grateful guests, but as the purview of that
aegis expands, the urgency of specifying what exactly one means by it in any
particular context increases proportionally. The term often seems to indicate
a hazy sense of approval ("poetry" is the name we give to texts we like) rather
than anything specifically descriptive (such as the Slavic Formalists' definition
of "language oriented away from the communicative function")—*poetry* is the
master term in a language of value. Accordingly, the same evaluative function
has seeped into subgenres as well, as if "avant-garde" or "conceptual" were a
badge of honor (forgetting Hugh Kenner's admonition that "the avant-garde
can be just as boring as anything else"). A language of precision, rather than
vague praise, would serve poetics well.

TIM FIELDER

from *Matty's Rocket*

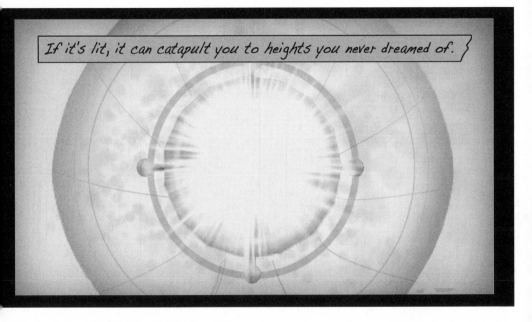

The Roper's Daughter

The pose that internalizes?

Death,
Standing on somebody's head.
—But clutch not
Even this.
Because
If the world dies
Nobody dies.

"The sky can't be fixed."

Then she laments—
"A voice
Inside me says
The truth—
Naked
Does not function."

But remember,
A telephone is ringing.
And before knowing
What to say—
It has been said.
"But please, sir—
Take my hand?"

The Roper's daughter
Engaged now
To a man who insists—

"Lies wipe the mind.
But to live in a powerful country
Is to be distant
From the river
Of all true feeling.
So I—Do nothing.
—For the surprise."

At that moment—
A triangle between you
—Looking at a woman being filmed,
And the camera doing the filming,
And the woman being filmed
—Who looks, now
Into the empty space
No one else occupies.

I. E. Mind on a rampage.

And wisdom
Elightens not
—But won't go away.

Head over heels
In abundance.

Oh, Oh!—the door of the ear
Wounding the body!

The Roper's Daughter saying
"Never wound
The Wound!
—If it's burning
Don't touch it."

Remember—
The Sky can't be fixed.

In Tongues

(for Auntie Jeanette)

1.

Because you haven't spoken
in so long, the tongue stumbles and stutters,
sticks to the roof and floor as if the mouth were just
a house in which it could stagger like a body unto itself.

You once loved a man so tall
sometimes you stood on a chair to kiss him.

2.

What to say when one says,
"You're sooo musical," takes your stuttering for scatting,
takes your stagger for strutting,
takes your try and tried again for willful/playful deviation?

It makes you wanna not holla
silence to miss perception's face.

3.

It ain't even morning or early,
though the sun-up says "day," and you been
staggering lange Zeit gegen a certain
breathless stillness that we can't but call death.

Though stillness suggests a possibility
of less than dead, of move, of still be.

4.

How that one calling your tryin'
music, calling you sayin' entertaining, thinks
there's no then that we, (who den dat we?), remember/
trace in our permutations of say?

What mastadonic presumptions precede and
follow each word, each be, each bitter being?

5.

These yawns into which we enter as into a harbor—
Come. Go. Don't. says the vocal oceans which usher
each us, so unlike any ship steered or steering into.
A habit of place and placing a body.

Which choruses of limbs and wanting, of limp
linger in each syllabic foot tapping its chronic c/odes?

Song

I want color to braid,
to bleed, want song
to fly to flex to think
in lines. To work
the pulp, to open up
this cardinal feeling
in green.

The hardest part
is the songbirds
and their fugue state,
fug state, fuck it.
The world is neon
in the gloaming quiet.

I am willing to walk
away, willing to be
on fire, to blaze
to Blake, to sink
into the moon's
aphorism and
its garden of figures.

The moon above
my life. It's rough
and real tonight,
cold fusion
reflecting sun.
There is a quaver,
a gibbous light
to this equation.

Puzzling rays full
of dinghies, pixies,
kobolds, and gems,
heroes, songsters,
and your face.
The strangeness
becomes you,
darling night.

JODY GLADDING

Five Poems

the spiders

what I mean

have been

by rooted

revising

my

is

full

of

my arms

laundry

lines

at the end of the   day

but

not taproot

web

old

stumps cling

with

all the

entanglements

the

hawthorn

came

into

flower

in

was

my

a

first

white

flame

turning

the

alphabet

to

kindling

59

family library

what it houses
the
spines
tapped
sometimes
leak
from my father's trees
hung icicles
nights
I've searched back
shelves
for a water glass
just
take these
he said
happens
I don't
read anymore

second
story window
cracked
open   room I've
been meaning
to finish
        half my
lightfe

many

were

left

unshelved

or leaned

a little

silently

browsing

old

remained

standing like horses

sleeping

against one another

after

the

books

libraries

closed

in

their

dark

stacks

61

why

because

womenan

first

wanted

ears

also

flared

from

her

the

whorls

of

her

temples

vulva

and

what

good

are

those

ears

did   first   woman   hear

listeners

lean closer

let me whisper it to you

from *Selected Tweets*

July

'Getting fetal' should be a thing people say refer-
ring to fetal position. Like 'I can't wait to go home
and get fetal after work today.'

Inside my cubicle, nobody can hear me scream

Sweat is useful in cooling you down and disguising
your tears

Suicide #lifehack

The cops let me keep my cocaine and fireworks.
God bless america

The only way to maintain relationships, I've
learned, is to lie to constantly and expect nothing
and act in ways that are unpredictable and insane

People only have sex with me to prove that they are
as depressed as they say they are

'Living' is just the longest and most painful form of
suicide

Was gonna tweet 'I accidentally got cornstarch in
my bangs' but what I really mean is 'I was experi-
menting with putting cornstarch in my bangs'

Don't ask me about my hair (I put cornstarch in it)

You only don't live past 30 once

'No old friends either'—Drake

A grocery store employee didn't know what Pop
Tarts were so he directed me to another employee
who also didn't know what Pop Tarts were

All this cocaine is going straight to my uterus

August

I told my roommate we should keep the mouse
because there's a pretty big chance it's actually a
very tiny dog

I want my funeral to be a pizza party with 500
pizzas and nobody is allowed to leave until all the
pizzas are eaten

Watching someone do pushups while I lay on my
stomach in a bed and eat a ~300 calorie piece of
cookie

Hello xanax my old friend

I'm the only person at da club with a yeast
infection

Gonna put 'depressed and selfish' under the special
skills section in my resume

September

'I'll just google the dosage'—famous last words

I'm AT LEAST an alcoholic1

Contrary to popular belief, drugs are, in fact, 'the answer'

Eating banana flavored klonopin and quietly rubbing myself on things

I just vomited at a place called 'Hot and Crusty'

Green eggs and help me

Everyday I'm sufferin'

Just whipped out my bag of kiwis on the subway platform and everyone was like 'Damn, check out THAT girl'

If you don't know how to be happy and you know it clap your hands

October

I will look back at this period of my life and think [abandoning this tweet, too grim]

'Too stupid to lie' is now a characteristic that I find sexually attractive

I did it all for the . . . (don't remember)

An extremely smelly homeless guy stumbled out of a liquor store then got really close to my face and said 'Hi, I'm the real Slim Shady'

I met a fun guy at the bus stop who likes my giant bottle of wine (I found some klonopin on my floor just now and ate it) #funguy

I'm looking to get carried out of Applebees on a stretcher tonight

What if shittier books were more flammable

I'm excited to have more time to play World of Warcraft and do cocaine alone in my room now that nobody is having sex with me

Had a dream that Parker Posey said to me 'There's a bank that doesn't have ATMs but business is booming because they sell turkeys for super cheap'

I'm high on cocaine and eating a burrito on a stoop in front of Planned Parenthood at 4:30pm on a Thursday

They're playing 'Ignition Remix' at Planned Parenthood

I wanna star in a porn movie called 'One Girl, One Macbook' (the porn involves me putting an entire Macbook in my vagina, I think)

Hating myself is my main bitch and hating other people is my side bitch

Relationships are like smoking crack. The
extremely euphoric high, then the comedown and
the horrible, inevitable, insatiable fiending

I don't actually enjoy parties or relationships, I
just like the idea that I could maybe be in either of
those things

Vague relationships where neither person wants to
feel comfortable or happy, that's that shit I used to
like

My milkshake makes all the boys run away to
Mexico . . .*

Today my editor said if he had a threesome with
me he wouldn't be able to get it up and I said
'Every threesome I've had ended in tragedy'

All the drugs are broken

Self help book titled 'How To Hate Other People
More Than You Hate Yourself'

An advertising campaign for the McRib says that
it has no bones, which means there is more pork,
which means there is 'more sandwich' . . . ?

I never clear my browser history after watching
porn but I'm really nervous about people hearing
me pee

If the only things that make you feel happy are
things that make you feel much worse in the long
term and you know it clap your hands

The main effect of all drugs is wanting more drugs

Spent Thanksgiving on a plane eating crackers so
high on xanax that I thought a poetry reading was
happening in the aisle

December

Today I ate 2 birth control pills because I like pills
and I have no self-control

'Life Is An Unbearable Nightmare No matter How
Much Raw Vegan Food You Eat' would be a pretty
name for a girl

Extremely stoned and incredibly stoned

I have PTSD from being an active participant in
my own life

The McRib really stresses me out

All I want for Christmas is infinite money and the
ability to reproduce asexually

The Unbearable Unavoidable-ness of Being

Ball so hard I somehow peed on everything but the
toilet

Yeah I'll fuck my cat, I'll fuck all your cats

If I eat a child will I become pregnant with
the child

I stand with the 50% of people in Iceland who
don't deny the existence of elves

Why does 2013 get to stop being a year but I have
to continue being Mira

---

*Tweeted this when my boyfriend flew from our home in New
York to Mexico immediately after I tried to break up with him.
Another boyfriend had done the exact same thing 2 months
prior.

Crux

Let's get it straight, they're employees, I'm the boss.

Edison grain, Himalayan salt.

Bars act as medicine men laying hands.

At contact, niggas are praying to maintain fans.

I'm prone to darker thoughts and Peter Parker witticism.

Known to target more than people guard the prison system.

When my carcass is burned and parked in an urn on a mantel, I'll still be
the hardest working, just a shift in prism.

Always been a prophet. Conjurer. Manifester better than, 100% of them.

Dammed to grip the pen in the hand of the better gender, so bending
letters better then gentlemen just presented the option of settling in.

Back of the bus relegated like Blacks slated.

The lady with crack laid in the pages.

Lack of phrases, never.

Hope that we're trapped in a cage together. Rorschach 'em.

Watch men approach and fall and tuck their balls back in.

Please . . . a vodka toast for every hour on the hour, so I don't go cop the
toast and Michael Douglas Falling Down 'em.

I'm a Kings County resider, with a bounty hunter mind inside her, with a
County Cullen kind of vibe to guide her.

Renaissance.

Polymath. Probably on my passing: iconoclast in mosques and synagogues
. . . now we into simpletons.

Been a cause, been a sin. Finnegan Begin Again.

Optimism was wearing thin, even on thicker keratin.

Huh . . .

The caring is a bearing, ain't it.

Can cause stress-related aging in immortal babies.

Morbid thoughts that separate you from your moral cause.

But serenading shouldn't maul the minds of born creatives.

That's why now I've got the gall of blonde girls with pom-poms with their mom's pearls at the prom with the promise of going to a good college to bond under a non scholarship and my dad's in the Klan and my family is into politics.

Bong.

I'll choke you with a tampon string.

Smoke over your body while some asshole sings.

I'm really not a part of your pardon, you're grasping . . . for mercy.

I don't have any personally. Ask him.

HOOK. (audible push ups, singing)

Who's always Rosewood pissed off, permanent bitch slaps,

Doing the Birdman hand rub in a 6-passenger van in the passenger seat and wearing a caftan, blaring the Gap Band covers of Scatman Crothers jams.

Unreasonable tin foil hat flow.

Rap so Blacks don't back peddle to crack hoes.

Motherland expat, Ex-Lax lexicon broad.

When I land, my jet's the Concorde.

Concourse J, bitch. No pedestrians on board.

Brontosaurus verse, ignoring the words to the chorus.

So your morals hurt more, like slipping on marbles on non-carpeted long-ass hall corridors.

Pall Mall smokes at a hole in the wall bar, sipping a long dark, flipping off all y'all.

That's all I got. Jokes and bars.

And I boast those dope, while you cope and co-star.

(I'm)

preying like a Space Ghost Coast to Coast star.

(I'm)

Ricki Lake in Lagos posting post cards.

(In)

Go carts at NASCAR, racing with blow darts.

Big, nigga. Zoltar. Nope. I don't spar.

I'm Carl and Michonne on my better days, I'll be in my Metamucil age refusing medicine, but letting men in to tend to my linens like, "Gentlemen, good evening . . . and following my bereavement is a team challenge."

Balance.

Valor.

Cadence.

Patience.

Manners.

Basic etiquette.

Relevant rhetoric brander.

Irreverent benevolent banter.

Callous.

Gracious.

Panoramic picture painter.

Realist.

Escapist.

Defendant, never plaintiff. I don't need to fucking claim shit.

I own shit. I'm old, shit. Jessica Tandy, Hume Cronyn shit.

Pepper in Annie. Get a home bitch.

Fuck outta mine. You the fuck outta line.

You don't even know how the fuck to rhyme, maroon.

Come on, yeah, goon. Call in the fuzz. Call in your cousins.

I want a run in. I'm fucking buzzed.

I've had a dozen ephedrines. I'll fucking lift trucks.

Crux of it, I'm Bugs Bunny with Dutch ovens on my knuckles and sans scruples and nan lovers.

So when the band tucks in and abandons the last dance, I'm the last motherfucker standing.

You don't wanna crash hands.

Lunactic——wait. I was trying to say lunatic brass . . . .

(ad libs out)

Okay, wait.

Lunatic brass pants . . .

from "death / is an / innumerable / accuracy"

```
                              to list
                                     at once  the sky
          the physical  being
                                            that   is
  as  form                                    is
  in   time
                                     everywhere
              as music                         is
                     in physical                 almost
                                     con-
                     form            sequential
                 the listing  takes

          as lost  or  left  or
                                            what canvas
                     when  wind  is
  time   only  in

                              con-
                     stellation
                                            there      when
          life   one   happens
                                     it
                 is   one
                                     cleaves
                     bound
                                            its imagination
                        sensor
                 serially
                                     to music
```

from "Amnicola"

Pali to *English*

river nadī (f.), gaṅgā (f.), ninnagā (f.), saritā (f.),
savantī (f.), āpagā (f.)
river-bank nadīkūla (nt.), nadītīra (nt.)
river-basin gaṅgādhāra (m.)
river-bed nadītala (nt.)
river-god nadīdevatā (f.)
river-head nadīpabhava (m.)
river-month nadīmukha (nt.)
riverain gaṅgāsanna (adj.), gaṅgāyatta (adj.),
` ` nadītīravāsī (adj.)

French to *English*

rivière + -ain "people living along a river"
Adjective: *riverain* m. (f. riveraine, m. plural
riverains, f. plural riveraines)
riverside (along a river)
Noun: *riverain* m. (plural riverains)

Latin to *English*

amnicolist: one who dwells by a river

Anagrams: riverain → vernirai
Verb, vernirai: first-person singular simple
future of vernir [to varnish]

Latin amnicola ("dwelling by a river") +
English – ist; compare the French amnicole
Pronunciation: ămnĭ´kəlĭst, IPA: /
æm'nikəlist/, SAMPA: /{m"nIk@lIst/
Noun: *amnicolist* (plural *amnicolists*)
(formal, rare) One who dwells by a river.

After last Ice Age, until 10,000 BCE, there
lived in Illinois a 300-lb beaver called the Gi-
ant Beaver, a 12-foot lion called the Ameri-
can Lion, the Smilodon a 620-lb saber tooth
cat 8 feet in length, the Wooly Mammoth,
a 10-foot sloth, the Grizzly Bear, Dire Wolf,
for 2000 years the Clovis people lived with
these animals.

These are a list of the nonhumans made
extinct or otherwise extirpated from Illi-
nois since European settlement. The Cot-
ton Mouse, extirpated, last captured in Illi-
nois in 1909. The Porcupine, barbed quills,
may have been extirpated before 1850. The
Timber Wolf, *Canis lupus*, extirpated, once
widespread in Illinois. *Felix Conqueroar*,
the Mountain Lion, extirpated 1900, largest
range of any mammal in North America.
The marten, *Martes americana*, extirpated,
last seen 1859, occupied north fourth of
state. The Fisher, cousin to Marten, *Mar-
tes pennant*, extirpated shortly after 1859.
Black bear, *Ursus americanus*, extirpated,
occasionally wanders in from neighboring
states. *Bos bison*, extirpated, once common
on Illinois prairies. *Cervidae* the American
elk, or *wapiti*, *Cervus elaphus*, extirpated,
ranged widely throughout state in early
1800s. However,

Praise be the Meadow Jumping Mouse, *Zapus hudsonius*, as it is common statewide and routinely leaps to one meter

Let the Thirteen-lined Ground Squirrel, *Spermophilus tridecemlineatus*, be acknowledged, as it is common and nearly half the year may be spent by it in hibernation

Note that the Beaver, *Castor canadensis*, is common statewide, despite hundreds of years of predation, once extirpated, and is the largest rodent in North America

Consider that the Northern Short-tailed Shrew, *Blarina brevicauda*, is common in the north 3/4ths of the south-central counties of the state, and that it is venomous and is the most abundant mammal in forested areas

Note that the Pygmy shrew, *Microsorex hoy*i, is uncommon in the northeast and southeast corners of the state and that it is the smallest mammal in the world

Consider that the Least Weasel, *Mustela nivalis*, is uncommon in the northern half of the state but is doing relatively well and is

---

[1](520 ILCS 5/2.2) (from Ch. 61, par. 2.2)

Sec. 2.2. This Act shall apply only to the wild birds and parts of wild birds (their nests and eggs), and wild mammals and parts of wild mammals that are hereby defined as follows:

All birds, both game and non-game (except the House Sparrow, Passer domesticus; European Starling, Sturnus vulgaris; and Rock Dove or Domestic Pigeon, Columba livia). GAME BIRDS— Ruffed grouse, Bonasa umbellus; Sharp-tailed grouse, Pediocetes phasianellus; Bobwhite quail, Colinus virginianus; Hungarian Partridge, Perdix perdix; Chukar Partridge, Alectoris graeca; Ring-necked Pheasant, Phasianus colchicus; Greater Prairie Chicken, Tympanuchus cupido;

the smallest carnivore in the world. Then
again here is a list of wild animals[1]

that have not been seen in Illinois since the
Chicago River was reversed:

Torpid Musket Snake, Translucent-shelled
Box Turtle, Stump-sized Emerald Lake
Snail, Excitable Northern Big-eared Turtle,
Deepswimming Wood Egret, Eastern Light-
ningball Crayfish, Lined Greater Snuffbox

Wild Turkey, Meleagris gallopavo. MIGRATORY GAME BIRDS—Waterfowl including brant,
wild ducks, geese and swans, Anatidae; rails, gallinules and coots, Rallidae; snipe, Gallinago
gallinago; woodcock, Scolopax minor; pigeons, including doves and wild pigeons (except
domestic pigeons), Columbidae; and crows, Corvidae. RESIDENT AND MIGRATORY NON-
GAME BIRDS—Loons, Gaviidae; grebes, Podicipedidae; pelicans, Pelecanidae; cormorants,
Phalacrocoracidae; herons, bitterns and egrets, Ardeidae; ibises and spoonbills, Threskiornithidae;
storks, Ciconiidae; vultures, Carthartidae; kites, hawks and eagles, Accipitridae; ospreys,
Pandionidae; falcons, including the Peregrine Falcon, Falconidae; cranes, Gruidae; rails and
gallinules, Rallidae; all shorebirds of the families Charadriidae, Scolopacidae, Recurvirostridae
and Phalaropodidae; jaegers, Stercorariidae; gulls and terns, Laridae; cuckoos, Cuculidae; owls,
Tytonidae and Strigidae; whip-poor-wills and nighthawks, Caprimulgidae; swifts, Apodidae;
hummingbirds, Trochilidae, Kingfishers, Alcedinidae; woodpeckers, Picidae; kingbirds and
flycatchers, Tyrannidae; larks, Alaudidae; swallows and martins, Hirundinidae; crows, magpies
and jays, Corvidae; chickadees and titmice, Paridae; nuthatches, Sittidae; creepers, Certhiidae;
wrens, Troglodytidae; mockingbirds, catbirds and thrashers, Mimidae; robins, bluebirds
and thrushes, Turdidae; gnatcatchers and kinglets, Sylviidae; pipits, Motacillidae; waxwings,
Bombycillidae; shrikes, Laniidae; vireos, Vireonidae; warblers, Parulidae; European Tree Sparrow,
Passer montanus; blackbirds, meadowlarks and orioles, Icteridae; tanagers, thraupidae; cardinals,
grosbeaks, finches, towhees, dickcissels, sparrows, juncos, buntings and longspurs, Fringillidae.
GAME MAMMALS—Woodchuck, Marmota monax; Gray squirrel, Sciurus carolinensis; Fox
squirrel, Sciurus niger; White-tailed jackrabbit, Lepus townsendii; Eastern cottontail, Sylvilagus
floridanus; Swamp rabbit, Sylvilagus aquaticus; White-tailed deer, Odocoileus virginianus. FUR-
BEARING MAMMALS—Muskrat, Ondatra zibethicus; Beaver, Castor canadensis; Raccoon,
Procyon lotor; Opossum, Didelphis marsupialis; Least weasel, Mustela rixosa; Long-tailed weasel,
Mustela frenata; Mink, Mustela vison; River otter, Lutra canadensis; Striped skunk, Mephitis
mephitis; Badger, Taxidea taxus; Red fox, Vulpes vulpes; Gray fox, Urocyon cineraoargenteus;
Coyote, Canis latrans; Bobcat, Lynx rufus. OTHER MAMMALS—Flying squirrel, Glaucomys
volans; Red squirrel, Tamiasciurus hudsonicus; Eastern Woodrat, Neotoma floridana; Golden
Mouse, Ochrotomys nuttalli; Rice Rat, Oryzomys palustris; Bats, Vespertilionidae.
  "It shall be unlawful for any person at any time to take, possess, sell, or offer for sale, any of
these wild birds (dead or alive) and parts of wild birds (including their nests and eggs), wild
mammals (dead or alive) and parts of wild mammals, including their green hides contrary to the
provisions of this Act."

Owl, Sleighbell Brook Frog, OtterToed Deer, Ornate Pallid Springfly, Horseleaping Pond Frog, Bladderlike Higgins Osprey, Threatened Plains Ribbonsnake, Very Little Bat, Lamprey Chub, Broad-handed Pugnose, Black-crowned Upland Least Northern Darter Snail, Ignitable Piping Snake, Robust Butterfly, Immensebodied Ashborer, Havocinducing Lake Fish, Timber Turtle, Pallid Owl, Eastern Black-eyed Fox, Disquieting Indianfriendly Eagle, Mississippi Taillight Hawk, Killifish Moorhen, Common Whistling Turtle, Ashley's Brook Shiner, Featherless Loggerhead Cardinal, Steam-colored Blanding's Harrier, Iowa-slow Mucket, Cypress-destroying Warbler, Bantam Mussel, Slough-loving Eastern Spotted Fritillary, Southeastern Kidneyshell Robin, Eastern Weed Rat, Regal Eastern Iowa Pimpleback Finch, Elfin Bigclaw Crow, Purple River Amphipod, Barn Salamander, Hog-Nosed Pocketbook Mouse, Cave Bluebrook Lampmussel, Snapping Black Pleistocene Coachwhip Crayfish, Mercurial Sandshell Rat, Porch-eating Amphipod, Spectaclecase Shrimp, Rafinesque's Striped Purple Pink Least Crayfish, Mississippi Longnose, Miniature Badger, Horsebloodying Watersnake, Mankindliking Bobcat, Orangefoot Sucker Shrike, Ohio Hydrobiid Tern, Forster's Stem Fanshell, Anomalous Indiana Turtle, Central Bluebreast Minnow, Peregrine Woodchuck, Swainson's Asocial Dragonfly, Awful Eryngium Watersnake, Sandloving Night-Heron, Waterbearing Sparrow, Eye-attacking

Bittern, Impatient Rabitt, Gravel Crayfish,
Redveined Erect Skipper, Oddlyveined Gav-
el-sized Bat, Pseudolunar Sunfish, Franklin's
Americanflag Sunfish, Rocksnail River Hen,
Elephant-eared Rail, Great Prairie Shin-
breaker, Least Lefteye Prairie Shinbreaker,
Cerulean Rabbitsfootshaped Hawk, Illinois
Swainson's Fogeschewing Hawk, Arrogant
Shawnee Toad, Phalarope Redhorse Snake,
Eastern-Moving Leafhopper, Bigeye Top-
minnow, Gray Silvery Shiner, Cave-Green
Lilliput Softshell Snake, Short-eared Shiner,
Railroad Butterfly, Yellow-headed Treefrog,
Pigtoe Tern, Ebonyshell Bat, Common-
brained Skipper, Illinois Muckpuppy,
Tern Skimmer, Ironcolored Hellbender,
Dusky Chub, Monoclewearing Mud War-
bler, Western Amphipod Frog, Featherless
Thorned Nuthatch, Timber Alligator, Wren-
following Wolf, Cave Kite, Bird-voiced Star-
head, Blackchin Clubshell, Mouse Squirrel,
Ground Black Bigeye Blackbird, Inkwant-
ing Salamander, Kirtland's Snake Lamprey,
Least Bitter Rattlesnake, Box Owl, Bedi-
zened Salamander, Massasauga Salaman-
der, Very Flat Salamander, Oily Flathead
Bewick's Salamander, Small Rainbowfind-
ing Salamander, Hine's Tern, Complete-
ly Yellow Turtle, Blacknose Cooter Killer,
Forestfly, Ricedepleting Springtail, Iowa
Riffleshell, Jeffersonian Metalmark, Red-
spotted Madonna, Northern Little Darter,
Elfin Sturgeon, Hoary Wilson's Scorpion,
Constantly Present Narrowmouth Falcon,
Obsequious Darter Rat, Night-Heron-kill-

ing Plover, Fluorescent Plains Heron, Importunate Cistern Salamander, Sturgeon Cuckoo, Ubiquitous Cobweblike Spotted Skipper, Noisome Horseleaping Town Fox, Kentucky Spring Wavy-rayed Chorus Fish, Reclusive Harlequin Common Slippershell Mini Turtle, Pompous Four-toed Sturgeon, Inconsiderate King Sandpiper, Boring River Salamander, Boring Karner Packard's Prairie-Chicken Shinbreaker.

Cotton Still Tops in Area Economy

The vote split almost completely along racial lines.

Little obelisk on bluff:

TOM LEE

A WORTHY NEGRO

"inculcation of racist ideology . . . inadvertent . . . happened
almost organically . . . "

The vote split almost completely along racial lines

In the Peabody lobby, around its marble fountain,
over mint juleps and ducks, Mason and Faulkner
delineated the beginning of the delta, north and south
Mississippi crackers cracked jokes about the Yankees,
who "put *sugar* on their *meat*"

The vote split almost completely along racial lines

" . . . an open detestation of things un-American
which essentially meant un-Memphian"
[which essentially meant un-white]

Your mission, should you decide to accept it, o favored son:
"give meaning & narrative coherence to Memphis."
(*Vaya con díos*)

The vote split almost completely along racial lines

"RACE-MIXING IS COMMUNISM":

" . . . a fearful growing race
once removed from the jungles.
My yardman went to his mother's
funeral in Mississippi. She had
104 grandchildren. How many
have you?"

The vote split almost completely along racial lines

In the '30s, the Cotton Carnival paid black men
to sit on cotton bales on street corners, play banjo,
perform the eating of watermelon—

a calvinist cotton-factor aristocracy's
version of carnival: no hierarchies inverted,
no relief from routine for the peasants, no
rituals of reversal here

                    among racial lines

if he has "the right attitude,"
if he comes with his hat in his hand
he may humbly beseech Us to "end the use of
the term 'n----r' on the police radio."

          split almost completely

"Memphis is beautiful with Spring, as you remember,"
with the azaleas and dogwoods flowering,
here & there, for some

Sources

"inculcation of racist": Kimberly K. Little, *You Must Be from the North: Southern White Women in the Memphis Civil Rights Movement* (Jackson: University Press of Mississippi, 2009), 11.

"put *sugar* on their *meat*": James Conaway, *Memphis Afternoons: A Memoir* (Boston: Houghton Mifflin, 1993), 20.

"an open detestation": Conaway, *Memphis Afternoons*, 125.

"give meaning & narrative": Wanda Rushing, *Memphis and the Paradox of Place: Globalization in the American South* (Chapel Hill: University of North Carolina Press, 2009), 6. "Memories and identities from the past and self-consciousness, pride, shame, and ambivalence about those identities give meaning and narrative coherence to Memphis as a distinctive southern place and shape place identity."

"Race-Mixing" and "A fearful, growing race": David M. Tucker, *Memphis since Crump: Bossism, Blacks, and Civic Reformers, 1948–1968* (Knoxville, TN: The U of Tennessee P, 1980) 133.

"In the '30s": Cf. Rushing, *Memphis*, 171.

"calvinist cotton-factor": Cf. Rushing, *Memphis*, 156.

"the right attitude" and "end the use of": Tucker, *Memphis since Crump*, 140.

"Memphis is beautiful": Conaway, *Memphis Afternoons*, 44.

from "Interventions: Notes on Translating *Intervenir*"
de "Intervenciones: Notas sobre el proceso de traducir *Intervenir*"

Write "my love's face in the dirt"
Write "what did they do to you, love?"
Write "I found my love's body missing a finger"

Translation is a form of dictation. You speak (in your writing). I listen (by reading). I listen further (by re-reading). And further (by writing which is re-writing). I speak (in writing which is a re-writing of what I read when I listen to your writing). You (writer of the original) tell me (writer of the translation) what to write.

This dictation is a form of intervention: the writing of the original intervened by the occurrences, vocabularies, and relations of the world; the writing of the translation intervened by the writing of the original, and by the occurrences, vocabularies, and relations of the shift in context that is the world of a text transposed elsewhere.

Escriba "el rostro de mi amor en la tierra"
Escriba "¿qué te hicieron, amor?"
Escriba "al cuerpo de mi amor lo encontré sin un dedo"

La traducción es una forma de dictado. Tú hablas (en tu escritura). Yo escucho (al leer). Yo escucho más (al re-leer). Y más (al escribir que es re-escribir). Yo hablo (al escribir que es un re-escribir de lo que leo cuando escucho tu escritura). Tú (escritxr del original) me dices (escritxr de la traducción) qué escribir.

Este dictado es una forma de intervención: la escritura del original intervenida por los sucesos, vocabularios y relaciones del mundo; la escritura de la traducción intervenida por la escritura del original, y por los sucesos, vocabularios y relaciones del traslado del contexto que es el mundo de un texto transpuesto en otro lugar.

The translator talks back to the dictation. The title of Dolores and Rodrigo's book is *Intervenir*, a verb in the infinitive: to intervene. The title of my translation is *Intervene*, a verb conjugated. A first person? A second person? A third person? Plural? Singular? An imperative?

Economy of language is central in this work, though the work has many centers and no center—it migrates, it falters, it refuses to be held, it resists. Part of the work of this translation was a practice of hewing, as in cutting to a congruently concise economy; part of the work of this translation was a practice of hewing, as in cleaving to the language channels this writing cuts into the terrain it traverses. A practice of conforming to the dictates of someone else's economy. A practice of necessity. A practice of pain.

*

Xl traductxr responde al dictado. El título del libro de Dolores y Rodrigo es *Intervenir*, un verbo en infinitivo. El título de mi traducción es *Intervene*, un verbo conjugado. ¿Una primera persona? ¿Una segunda persona? ¿Una tercera persona? ¿Plural? ¿Singular? ¿Imperativo?

La economía de lenguaje es central en esta obra, aunque ésta tiene muchos centros y ninguno—migra, titubea, se niega a ser contenida, resiste. Parte del trabajo de esta traducción fue una práctica de *hewing*, de tallar, en el sentido de cortar para alcanzar, en congruencia, una economía concisa; parte del trabajo de esta traducción fue una práctica de *hewing*, en el sentido de atenerse a los surcos que esta escritura cava en el terreno que atraviesa. Una práctica de ajustarse a los dictados de la economía de alguien demás. Una práctica de necesidad. Una práctica de dolor.

ERICA HUNT

Should You Find Me

Should you find me, I'm the short one on the left, knocking brown against green hills, a fleck in the crowd, not to be blinked on or peeled, coming off with the tape.

Should you find me, would you have a word for me, or do I go forward on faith for a new word, different spelling.

Where would you find me? At the top of residential grids, in the tear downs and the private cul-de-sacs, or at the bottom, in the nameless streets, pavement dwellers tapping into the futility lines for brown-out power?

Where would you find me? Which kidnap do you mean, you ask? In security chambers, handcuffed, soundless zeroes maximum cancellations of futurity? In the malls' maw thrall of fear-numbing card-bearing youth? Or in abandoned villages smoking ruins patrolled by Uzi-besotted soldiers? When the codes change, does the energy suck remain the same?

Would I recognize my name in the voice calling from the burning bush? Would I hold my breath and hope it wasn't me, and if it isn't me who else will carry the tune?

If you should find me, would I have to relearn my own name, talk to the letters in the alphabet, one by one, my new best friends? Would I have to invent spill over: there's got to be more days in the year, birthdays shouldn't be rationed, we need new shoes, we need to replace perpetual war footing?

If you should find me, does that mean the pop quiz in the picture—rebus times pantomime tariffs pygmy? Would I button down? Do fewer wrinkles in the forehead automatically lead to new wrinkles in the knees?

If you should find me, could I stop doing, doing, doing red onions, beets, radishes, peppers? Then who would restore the color to crunch? Everyone knows it's not easy to hold things still: the red and its expectation, the bell and its clapper, the beet to its sugar.

Should you find me, how could I miss? Who would I miss? Who would miss me?

If you should find me, I would measure as it has taken time to learn how, practice a long view: the pinch, a pause, punctuation in the moment.

Light Headed

If I were less civilized,
I'd sit on a mountain of green bowlers
manufactured in China
out of cheap plastic,
your grave markers,
with your pale lifeless bodies
strewn about the foothills,
impaled on jagged rocks.
I'd grimace like a bleached skull
with the sun glinting in a blinding yellow brilliance
off the metallic surface
of my gold-capped teeth.
Maybe I'd laugh long and loud,
wearing a sparkling pair of red patent-leather shoes
with pointed toes.
Welcome to Red Congo Square.
The location
on the Map
is blossomed
with my blood.

Self-Portrait as Shop Window

After David Rivard

On the bus

Thus the passing parade—All Hallow's Eve

Winds swing the hoop skirt beneath the milk maid's dress
Of the little white girl complete with Marie Antoinette
Mold on cheek

While into central Brooklyn, the costumes are home
made—the best a young blood
In Diaper—complete with pins—Oh, P. Funk or Red Hot Chili Peppers

Cheekbones apparent & a rivulet of veins
Rhymes with what—plains, gains, claims, trains

Bus stops & the texting children act as sentinels
Letting us off or on as they please

I have often mistaken the mocking bird for an owl
It's a problem I cannot solve. There are other ones, more difficult.

I listen again for the bird's call. It's mocking me. There seem
To be cows in Roethke's poems and birds in mine. Nature is
ever present even unto this great city that grumbles and crumbles
And yet allows the mocking bird's song and hummingbird's wings

to flash like a taste of the cosmos. Oh damn the wind and light
Or praise the rain and bright desire for different weather. I stand

in front of these beautiful things and curb my appetite for murder.

ERICA KAUFMAN

[how speech might help]

how speech might help
loss how our doubts seem

richer how code shifting
should not be severe

how we're all intrinsically
valuable how there's always

a way to connect how
glaciers are more than

a giant hunk of ice how
articulate how operational

how rigorous how am i
still driving in the midst

of so many inches
of hypothetical snow

Elegy for Harold Ramis

Oh! You're here. Oh, this is big, Peter. This is very big. There's definitely
something here. It's moving! It's here. It's a woman. Ready. I wouldn't say
the experience was completely wasted. Based on these new readings, I think
we have an excellent chance of actually catching a ghost and holding it
indefinitely. I'm always serious. Just for your information, Ray, the interest
payments alone for the first five years come to over $75,000. It's 9,642.55
square feet. Our courteous and efficient staff is on call 24 hours a day to
serve all your supernatural elimination needs. Print is dead. Is that a game?
I collect spores, molds and fungus. I think it's the food of the future. She's
telling the truth—or at least she thinks she is. Or even a race memory,
stored in the collective unconscious. And I wouldn't rule out clairvoyance
or telepathic contact either. You're a Scorpio with your moon in Leo and
Aquarius rising. Did you see anything? I blame myself. We'd better adjust our
streams. Something was definitely here. Were you recently in the bathroom?
The wet towels, residual moisture on your lower limbs and hair, the redness
in your cheeks indicating . . . When you were in the bathroom, did you notice
anything that was yellow and unusually smelly? Ray! Where are you? Are you
all right? Ray! It's here! It just went into the Banquet Room on the third floor.
Wait! Wait! There's something I forgot to tell you. Don't cross the beams. Trust
me. It will be bad. It's hard to explain, but try to imagine all life as you know
it stopping instantaneously and finding yourself confined forever in another
dimension. Don't cross them! Watch it! Easy . . . Easy . . . I'm going to throw
in my trap now. He's in here. They're not guns. They're particle throwers. I
couldn't do that. You might hurt someone. On Earth—no. But on Krypton
we could slice him up like Oscar Mayer Bologna. Neutronize. System shut.
I've got to sleep. I'm worried, Ray. It's getting crowded in there. And all my
recent data points to something big on the bottom. Well, let's say this Twinkie
represents the normal amount of psychokinetic energy in the New York area.
According to this morning's PKE sample, the current level in the city would
be a Twinkie 35 feet long weighing approximately six hundred pounds. Bring

him inside, Officer. I am Egon, Creature of Earth, Doctor of Physics, Graduate of MIT. Yes, have some. Vinz, what sign are you waiting for? Hello? What is it? Does she want to be? Some. I just met the Keymaster. He's here with me now. Venkman? Are you there? I agree. All right. I'll try. All right, Peter. Good night. Die in what sense? I don't care. I see us as tiny parts of a vast organism, like two bacteria living on a rotting speck of dust floating in an infinite void. You have nice clavicles. I wonder where Stantz is. I think we're going to need him. You can see what's inside through the monitor if you wish. He wants to shut down the storage grid. No . . . no water. There's nothing you can do. The storage facility blew. This one . . . shut off the protection grid. Oh, shit! If you don't shut up I'm going to rip out your septum. And look at this, Peter. Cold-riveted girders with selenium cores. Of course! Ivo Shandor, I saw his name in Tobin's SPIRIT GUIDE. He started a secret society in 1920. Yes. After the First World War Shandor decided that society was too sick to survive. And he wasn't alone. He had close to a thousand followers when he died. They conducted rituals, bizarre rituals, intended to bring about the end of the world. Who? You talked to Gozer? Sumerian—not Babylonian. What is it? I don't believe in luck. Thank you. It's Shandor—the architect! Not necessarily. I think he's saying that since we're about to be sacrificed anyway, we get to choose the form we want him to take. That appears to be the case. No. Full-stream with strogon pulse. No! Them! Shoot them! Cross the beams. Life is just a state of mind.

from *Civil Bound*

::

pity doves

silicate

the Great Lakes

slit   silt   syllabaries

::

as the skull disengages

as as would comes out capital

::

volubly, an ambush of human devotion

::

It is conceded that an interoceanic canal through any of the isthmus passes of the western hemisphere is a necessity for the present or prospective commerce of the world.

With the advantages of modern science, a canal can be built anywhere involving only the question of expense, provided water can be found to fill it.

September 26, 1870

::

circumpolar

rifles at the ready, aimed
next to
distribution of sacks of ground corn

::

Great Lakes stations

Port Washington, WI   1930–1981
Deluth, MN   1939–1981
Chicago, IL   1933–1978
Buffalo, NY   1935–1981
Rogers City, MI   1922–1987
Lorain, OH   1933–1981

::

ob /   s/r

debris architecture

persons to appear   97
persons who made

from *Glossary*

ANDROGYNE

express   outside

the   Other

ASEXUAL

which

we   face

like
what

CISSEXISM

so
oppression

HOMOPHOBIA

, ,

.

, /

, ,

.

(' ').

, ,

.

LIBIDO

In essence
can   ignore

LITHROMANTIC

it
fades

OUTING SOMEONE

Accidentally   intentionally

emo

PANGENDER

shade

QUEER

and

history as   slur

SEX-POSITIVE

ve movement is an ideolog
ions of sexuality are viewed as
orces as long as they remain conse
movement   ation and
its camp   kes no mo
tions amo   insert   ivities, regu
choices as   preference.
s are sex-   possible
o be repu   rsonal l
ositive towards humanity as a wh
so promotes the ability to d
erson does not want wit
sexual choices

TRANSVESTIC FETISHISM

i
D   o   n   t

ZUCCHINI

zucchini   platonic

XXIII

A tsunami enunciates its temper; its affect acts on fronts. Helios' stags have thrown their crown into the chill; seafarers fear rises. Puddles trouble stateside merchandisers' partners. Storms set fires, force ethics; NGOs reply et cetera with automaton ouch reagents who compose strife into great hysterical boundary panic. News freaks, chickens. Shitshows run The Earth. Solar information fuels a pyro future, a lust for ghettos, shady math. Depressed surfers beach totally epic buyers' remorse. Haenyo follow waves right into ocean-drilling luminescence; drowned lovers strewn along the sand teem with wormy decay. Hot merch cargos sidewind in the burning therm, minor famines billow and alight, movers shake midnight oil. An etymology of global smog speak is begun, but when the eloquence and dumbed prescience of aboriginal elders is proofed, memory speaks in globs of real shit. When people avoid afrorealist groove, blandness loops duckfaces over record temperatures. Defenses morph into euthanasia. Take that, atmosphere. Penguins, take that! Tremors ripple heat; thermometers measure exec pressure; dollars earn exoneration. Rivers bloated with waste slide lethargically into shallow graves, heat howls, spirit touches an arid winter. Three-eyed sibyls eloquently guess at oil proverbs' final little twist.

XXXIII

Free music lulls many angry, tailored-suited youth. Some mornings, the avenues bristle when flâneurs mutter under their custom foulards; the fountains stop: swish-clothed street lovers keep plugging into audile cyberspace, blocking the polis' chorusing whirl. The gay, bold, mean-faced theatrics of meanderers and widowers grants gentlemen gilded standing; on pedestals they stand, dreaming address with heavenly adolescents. Their myspace nostalgia can permutate into Spotify fetishes if bass pleasures are met. Soundclouds float above transit riders' worn outfits; thugly rackets wonh-wonh in streetcars' packed aisles. Palatial factories are renoed; lofty rooms with retrofits, tongue-and-groove floors, and walk-in closets draw lads; rough industrial visages hide sensitively aligned designer sound systems. Bearded downtown aesthetes wink at hot hipster ladies, Instagram charitable events, omg at boys in uniform, learn lines by black rap lyric masters to earn cred with kids. Their shiny bikes with brass bells, their Triumphs, make noisy streetscapes. Listeners endeavour to earn money by growing handlebar mustaches for full-time jobs at blacksmithesque wearhouses, but only scarce hourly minimum wages do they score. Plugged into online clouds, while apathy masks hide their misfortunes, some men discover Wild Style. Those hip hop mofos were the hippest, mixing vinyl on vintage turntables, in ghettos whitefolk disdained. The suburban sons of bitches who overlord municipal folky festivals entertain wishes involving heavy metal frontmen, substances, and gun-straddling angels of death.

LVII

Offline, I still believe in reading, in poetry, in slow culture. On social media, am I visible? What should I do but aim to trend? I use an app to manage the hours of absentminded time I spend scrolling fruitlessly down curated desires, but I have no sense of precious time at all once my attention locks into the opendlessness of streaming services. The story doesn't end; a serial-like storyness is our new questish narrative. In antistory, how do I dare? Millenial children know the world-without-end as hoax; the future whiles away, as governments bargain money and sovereignty against water's cleanliness. The atmospheric clock lurches forward and only stories without conclusion pretend a soothing. The kinesthetic, birthed tenderness of reading bodies tries patience: as our wishes unyoke our heads' aggressive ambition from the body's hour-servant condition, we bid the creaturely adieu. I want to read a realizing, the antiquest, a post-conclusion, wrighting in cursive hand my jealous thoughts and wishes (censored from my online automatism) into an energy, an embodiment, of the storyteller's punctuation. The caesurae of my feed, those unassuming bars of #d8dfea between squares of people's posts, imperceptibly iron out the lived kinesis, the abrasive and gesticulative beats that say beast, glandular, earthling. Like a chute of never-enough, the smart devices' downrush of personalized clickworthy is our appetite's groove, a hangry flow channel. People. There is a y and another y in this procedure. I make these poems from text's ulterior matter. Upstream, if you have followed this line woven through bardic tapestries, denotify your network. Your will endures through your reading. You make the unstory of this english sonneteer, this kink, snagging loops in the scrolls of influence.

No modernism

No modernism
No no moernism
Crusht dough
Slung than a minnows
A minnow climate conscious of
No not one single ne
Modernism no
Modernism bebeee write it on the
Bulletin boards baby the bulle—the fukn
rector's silhouette's deimension's
dilution creepeth up
Upon ye
Modernism noooo-oh-oh-oh none
Please no of modernist procliv
None provlic 'ward
Number 6ixxxx check that
Cashed-open CHOV bebeee
DEAD sober
Modernism please with a fen you
Ate gerund witch
Glean down your face to understand
Tumours which can
Split yon lobes till you
Cry strate down the mind!
Strate down the mind!
Bebeee this become
"Becoming-modernism" opening out nto glib
Staez of One
Thousand democracies cooperating up a STORM
It ell you ant yet done witnessed

Cooperation FRENZY that dem-oh
Smearing up bside your god
Dam nek
Shearn hornwise hine the earèd non, lobe have you
Have you deja entendéed à propos
Bout the aforementioné
Earèd lobes??
The moon   's-requested
tlefield where it charmed
Shits a BATTLEfield beb resistane to
pottery's a chattel
And we need one thing Modernism ta
Steer us envers
munchablest pastures!?/
no mor modern anythings no
Nunathat thems pessimist every
exterior smoking lst
Last wunavem pessimists your dial up
Momed gonna save the warld thank
God for ur stoic lyric marx
Cincheed up cigarette chaming
Than you in the reality external
Thank go for you
Thank fucking god for ur poems bra

Soprano Part for *Impromptu*

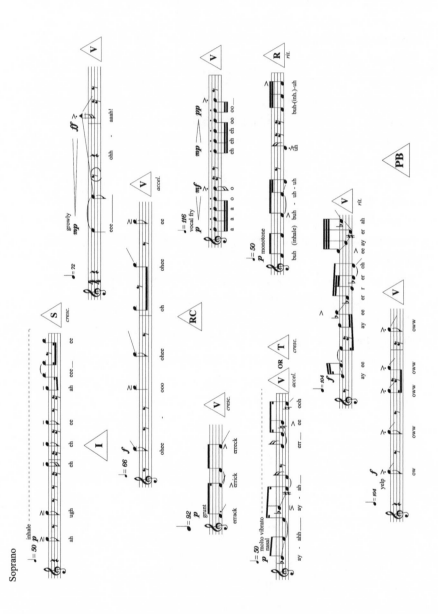

621B

Forgetting that reading wastes time is one of the cardinal sins of book reading. Forgetting you are reading [a book] is the other. Thus, the puzzle of shelf-life returns to haunt a book [management system], which do not disappear the moment after one looks at it, like digital billboards or text messages, or disperse information efficiently like memos or standardized forms. Workaround: read a book with a digital device nearby. As any poet can tell you, the function of words is to produce and regulate (i.e. ornament) our moods, and the most interesting poetry today is modeled on office productivity suites. All poems, like software, are systems for counting. Poets of earlier dynasties counted syllables; today, they parse text strings and tabulate character arrays.

Such tabulations are hardly novel. Homer's Odyssey transmitted historical data. Ezra Pound's injunction to make it new in re-versioned primers such as his ABC of Reading links poetry to news dissemination. Genres condition reading, and genres (take sheep-herding poetry) wear out, and they do so in particular mediums. Who reads eclogues or bucolics by Theocritus? Georgian war poetry circa 1904 feels irrelevant today, but so does lyric poetry in the Paris Review. Computational poems in PPT, where the genre known as the PPT presentation dissolves into something literary—may be another matter. Milton's Lycidas is notably mixed; it splits pastoral with elegy, and before it's done the form threatens to turn itself inside out. No surprise: today, instead of the pantoum, we have the Tumblr log or mixed verse of PowerPoint. A recourse to Delphic hymns and music in the chapel may be helpful: reading is a performance; a text is a score to be performed. As T.S. Eliot noted, "the poet has, not a 'personality' to express, but a particular medium, which is only a medium and not a personality."

Buck Moon

Getting laid on a <u>full moon</u>
for the first time in months
reminds me of all the times
I almost (died) from <u>pills</u>, and <u>sex</u>
But I <u>didn't</u> die, I ate a pill
and got laid on a full moon

HOOVES

Imagine if I had hooves
for teeth

would my mother love me?

or imagine if an angel
(appeared) ———————→ with three eyes
and a silver tongue

If she said everything
would be ok

would you believe
it?

When I die
I will watch

over you

I will amplify your
tongue

and your eyes
will be drag races

I will give you
electric

TEETH
teeth made of hooves

This kind of
dancing

is silent

Do you understand
what I say

when I grit my teeth teeth teeth teeth
ee
ee
ee
ee
eeee
eeeeee eeee
eeeeeeee eeee
and sleep?

Imagine if Matt
came back

with six heads
and tourniquets hanging

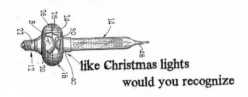

like Christmas lights
    would you recognize   **him**

    as an angel
        or would you be afraid   from the dripping
                                           silver

110   needles splayed
        FIG. 1 out   and everybody
                                      silent

When I die FIG. 2
    I will watch   the world burn
                          and I will

come back
    to burn   in its
                         place

burn burn burn burn burn burn   burn burn burn burn

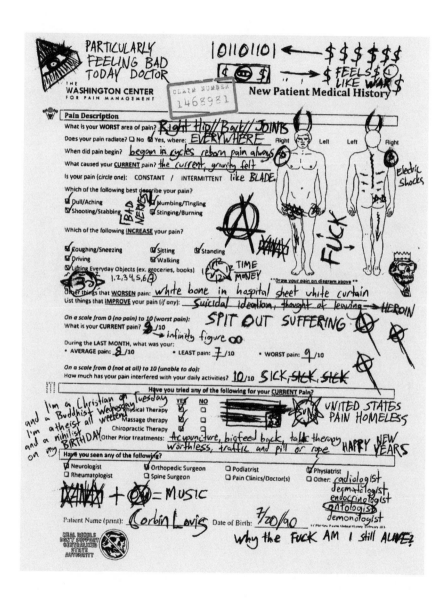

PSYCHOSOMATIC? ⟶ neuropathic?
⟶ structural deformity???
Or a tree uprooting itself

SURGICAL HISTORY

Please list all prior surgeries: **YES, A LOT**   ☐ I HAVE NEVER HAD SURGERY

WISDOM TEETH
all that pain and money
all that pain and money
all that Money

Surgery	Date (Approx.)	Left/Right (if applicable)
Inguinal Hernia	2011 Winter	LEFT
Ganglion Cyst	2013 FALL	LEFT is death
Septoplasty	2013 WINTER	
Arthroscopic Hip Surgery	2014 Summer	LEFT

Family History

List medical history for your **BIOLOGICAL** parents only.

☐ I HAVE NO SIGNIFICANT FAMILY MEDICAL HISTORY
☐ FAMILY MEDICAL HISTORY NOT AVAILABLE (adopted or no records)   BODY STOPPED

	Alcoholism	Cancer	Diabetes	Drug Use	Headaches	Heart Disease	High Blood Pressure	Osteoporosis	Rheumatoid Arthritis
Mother						✓	✓		
Father									

Other Conditions (please list): *Parents are resentment, boiling red, blood, almost over*

SOCIAL HISTORY   **SOCIAL REJECT//DOA//SMILE**

Are you currently employed? ☐ Yes ☑ No What is your occupation? *deadbeat/junky/coward/saint*
If not currently working, when did your last work? *spring time was a depression, was high*
Are you on disability? ☐ Yes ☑ No, If, Yes, since when? **DENIED** Why? **NO STATE SUPPORT**
Marital Status: ☑ Single *undateable* ☐ Married ☐ Divorced ☐ Widowed ☐ Other: _____
Number of Children: 0
Education completed: ☑ High School   ☐ Some College   ☐ Technical School   *school and*
☐ College Degree   ☐ Post-Graduate   ☑ Other (Please specify): *hospital is box*

Tobacco, Alcohol & Illegal Substances History

☐ I have never used tobacco
☑ Former Tobacco User: #Cigarettes or Packs/Day: **11 CIGS**   Quit Date: **2012**
☐ Current Tobacco User: #Cigarettes or Packs/Day: _____

GOOD BOX

Alcohol Use: ☐ Never ☐ Rarely ☐ Socially   ☐ Daily ☑ History of Alcoholism   ☐ Current Alcoholism
Illegal Substances:

HISTORY WHISKEY BROKEN MOUTH

consciousness is a spiral

Do you have a History of Illegal Substance Use? ☑ Yes ☐ No
Do you have a History of IV Drug Use? ☑ Yes ☐ No
Have you ever abused prescription medications? ☑ Yes ☐ No
Have you ever been in a detoxification program? ☑ Yes ☐ No   2014
Name of Program: **FAIRFAX HOSPITAL** When? **2014**
Substances Tried with Date of Last Use:
☑ Heroin **2012**   ☑ Cocaine **2015**   ☑ Marijuana **MANY TIMES**
☑ Methamphetamine **2011**   ☑ Other ████ *acid, mushroom, molly, OXY,*
Ketamine, Salvia,

Behavioral Health

Have you ever seen a psychologist/psychiatrist? ☑ Yes ☐ No
Diagnosis: **BIPOLAR II**   When? (Approx.) **2014**
Have you ever planned suicide? ☑ Yes ☐ No When? **NOW**
Have you ever attempted suicide? ☑ Yes ☐ No When? **BEFORE**
History of sexual abuse during childhood? ☐ Yes ☐ No When? _____

Psychic 333

Patient Name (print): **1468981**   Date of Birth: **Was Mistake**

Pain was a bible. Pain was a repitition. body repeat visceral. body repeat body. sistine Chapel. How it cracks still beautiful. Doctor said damaged nerves DO NOT HEAL. Doctor said unclear. Another surgery. i want to save myself.

JANICE A. LOWE

Boy Flower
Tamir

Headlines

Father rap *sheeeeit*!

Mother presses conference

Sister Wrestled to Ground

whi**p**

    la**sh**

lash

   ba**ck**

Tamir grew ?

Question mark wants to know *when*

around violence

Flower Boy in the View Finder

boy flower by-the-lake

his violet weediness

the chlorophyll of him

park innards

A growing green

heirloom boy

heritage seedling of the Western Reserve

Boy

Boy

ritual

streamed

in digital

pixelated

bits

sacrificial bytes

mother father sister

no memory enough

a shaming

a *taming*

a killing

Wannabe
Headline

Rogue

humanists

offer alternate

ways to look at

black boys

a different kind of imaging

anything else

air softing

`````````~~~~~racing grass

growing shy

or mouthy

growing out of shoes

ellipsis

## In View

land banks

urban preserves

# tree planting
# parties
## Family Swim

monitored

vacant edges

<u>Other exciting activities</u>

## Fitness
# watershed

## In the Viewfinder

An "isn't he cute" a lion cub

club

privileged hunter

play gamer

A shaky cop

## <u>LUNCH</u>

::::::::::::::

::::::::::::::

## Search

Cudell Rec in summer

Sundeck        Sauna

Game room      gym

## BASEBALL
## A*q*u*a*c*i*s*e

Water gains weight

If you enjoy the outdoors

Permission slips
`````````

SCHEDULE

"and pointing it at people.
Probably a juvenile, you
know? . . . I don't know if it's
real or not, you know?"

911 caller said he's
scaring the expletive out of
inaudible

police
car stops
at 0:19 by
0:21 the boy

is ground

Claim Rice failed to put his
hands   up

Hospital rush

day child mortally wounded

Sunday expired
The boy Tamir

Edge of water
gone

Think July and

firepower

working

too damned well

a time ago
Euclid Beach
Aero Dips
Racing Coaster
Flying Turns
The Thriller

Question Mark

they are lovely   did Rice grow up around violets
violins   Severance Hall   the orchestra
he was a **V** not for victory but velocity
question mark

cultural garden called weediness

period

wildfast

Natural History
identifies 136 tree
and plant species; 46
species of sedges,
grasses, mosses,
ferns and fungi; 56
**bird species; seven
amphibian and
reptile species; six
mammal species;
and 89 insect and
arthropod species**

violets

in the midwest are removed

or sprayed

or transplanted from native
beds to edges

will eventually cover lawns and
create a monoculture

remove wild strawberries
from traffic areas because
they tend to die and leave

muddy patches

Re: violets and strawberries
Have you found that they get too pushy
over time and shouldn't be encouraged?

purple violets growing in mostly full sun   white violets in
partial shade

in the mosaic of grasses
they can handle some mowing and foot traffic

I don't see any reason that you can't encourage them

exotic species
watch out

Nov. 26th article

history

justification

domestic

question mark

violins

mother *and* father

Cudell Corns Park
streamline
keep your readers hooked

Write a Review

Upload a photo

A recording
violins

Only in Cleveland

He was living in a gang
infested neighborhood
confirms he was a gangster

Cleveland Hopes

*Who shoots a
12-year-old from 10
feet away and expects
a free pass?*

Violet dreams

modesty

fortune

death too soon

soon too

Color Theory purple

confidence

Ballistic Eyes   power intuition

hitting each other with non-mental spheres

Floriograph   intuition

The orange tip   candor

how to distinguish airsoft guns from real firearms

innocence   if white shows

Euclid Beach Park Riot

protests 1946

"no sitting, no talking, no mixing of any kind ... between the races"

Congress of Racial Equality (CORE) put out by park police

Lynn Coleman and Henry MacKey intervene

They are Black cops   off-duty

Fight

Coleman was shot

with his own gun

(see below)

Cleveland Hopes

See below

An officer shot a kid

That is the issue

from www.theuse.info

the intro (or dont you have a phone?

al rang, wants his numbers back, (a, aThough whats there to gEt, it takes eighty people to Own half the facts of the world, the rests just insUrance .. the nExt word then, um, How to (you really dont want to know (an echo of coping (a mouthful of pistemology (And sEarch, (its user a type of Battery, all OnOff Functionality and bad sIgnage (you can tell its signage coz its been subjected to criteria (you knOw, one those credulous mirrors ofThe pAtient cures the subject (the curator of these selfsame clients) by paying him attEntion, poor thing. (theory is a crap prophylactic. all quack, no Handle. (.. it was better as an idea, (worrying the mic being invariably cheaper than the manufacture of instrumental reason, (it is of course illegal to imagine work without a lIcensing agreement or IV Number of some kind, .. though depends how you spell, Reify (the privatisation of my privacy by a rorschach other than mine (also known as Art, (Profit is superstItious, one of the mincy perks ofAnd Narrative is obviously driven Mad by being a fiction (the Hero, not so much. (i mean what language means to Say here (poetry confesses me her Therapist (or target (anyway one of the T words (every tax has their own silence (which is slightly constrained by being the main argument against documentation, (i mean sure, its in Dialogue with truth, but if we accept the past as an attempted self cure, whats the fucking chOice? a handwringing whitewashed lack of imagination (the user being its Content, not its crUsh, its unsatisfied wIfe (a lynch mob of One, (reproduction being just a critique of Context (context being that which will recognise a Question (hence a way of falling in love with the answer (with exclusive rights to billings of the New, (i mean basically a words just an hysteric of ancestor snatching, a sort of picture book of how to survive your nEeds, so, It, the poppy ambIvalent (context is forever skeptical (and coz it Rhymes (with, whateverthefuck, (coz it doesnt do tIme, (the fact is the self cure for which the fact is its Compromise (a charmingly Graceless compromise, but a story nonetheless, (i mean embarrassment is not necessarily a measure ofI mean in the last ten thousand years, the human brain shrank Eleven Twelve percent, so wefFor Example, (it illuminates duration, Actually just Like the bloody jokes and get On with it.

then theres the NSA (the role of an object being to organise silence), a platform Standard, (agreement was an experiment. lasted til they got a word for it, (i mean information is a type of measure of what could only have been Otherwise. its a metric of, Potential Difference, admits neither cloning nor indistinguishable states, (not even the residual nonlocal the sIde effect, (a cat is one end of a quantum computer, the rat is the other.

.. does the stone experience gravity as information, as Habit maybe, Theory, a form of Consciousness? a Predicate? a Loophole? a Generic loophole? is it fair to describe this as, understAnding? as, German? .. Ode to the Metaphysics of computation (inputs outputs and bAnking,

.. suggEsts identity (even though it looks like a form), exhibits intEnt (its neurotic (reproduction being its entIre argument (i mean if the storys not self identical and your neighbours wife belIeves that its not self identical then youd prob do better with a glue stick or a, dOg ..

in economics, the past devours the future and the rest is gas and in politics its the other way round. Being but, is Always a part of something Else. (i mean Wholes obviously fail to exist, (Negatives on the other hand both exist and Dont, so if youre going to model, Illness say, Thats obviously the way to gO. (Data, the study of immunology. (and Games, Dont forget the gAmes

.. (though how do they feel about being domesticated? (i mean a Fact thats been domesticated is clearly a slUt .. (ive come across disingenuous pauses in my time, but .. a pragmatic pantie Rental. i mean its just more efficient if not Everything has to be right.

.. what would identity be if it wasnt ideal? and would it Fit? like Proof? (.. Proof, you knOw, porn for Virtual Profit. (.. its in a domain of quantification so must be an, Object, (this is not a statement about Fish, (i mean a paradox is not an Object. (then it hits Puberty. (which doesnt mean that its, pOssible. Does but mean it relates to an Impossible in a particular wAy .. like, like incompleteness argues that the question deprIves itself of its object, and Yes, existence is a form of enlightenment (i mean talk about fUcked .. (flatlining is clear the prettier option. lofi lobotomy.

a patchy fact on valium, (.. not much of an intervention, i'll grant, but it .. probably better as a hack. slapstick for Cash. .. so whereSomewhere around the eleven minute mark?

.. some facts just sit around all day play the ricochet game, (as though Object was a, Lesson of some kind, not just a mere function ofWants toPain i means def cUte, (.. like a poets really just a Comments troll too serious to actually Sell you anything, (i mean All finance is synthEtic, a caps lock Cognitive vaccIne, so the takeaways are pretty much the sAme ..

argument by Debt (the userclient model Temp, the mechanPrice (you know, that which has been drained of capital), the maninthemiddle thirdparty anAlysis, a library of unrecognised passwords and lists and (.. actually, thatd be better as, English, or, This, as a libraryofunrecognised passwordsandlists, but .. (like, you need Me toI mean i'm flattered and all, but .. (Nature of course has its Own immune system (much to the popes surprise we're not It (so much for privacy, (or didnt the pope teach you how to score, how to account for the wrong question, bootstrap Vulnerability, the credulous sphinctered failure that is noIse, the knotting vOwel, the rented Witness (Cash, the stuttering accidents Of. (and as Any child will explAin, cain was of course not guilty coz no one knew blahblah what Death was, (it was this very innocence which allowed him then to invent the vicarious art ofThe perp Always turns out to be some unemployed News monger.

a word, a lump in the throat, an understAnding (the argument that time swings both ways, a hiccup of digital do-overs andArt (basically an ad avoiding eye contact, the sardonic strangely impoverished bourgeois timeandmotion study the Limpid fIb (its in the wrong tax bracket to be taken as a lIe, or even a decEption (facts being but glitchy mascots withI mean itd be more reasonable to accuse, the, wAlls of lying .. (what mum'd call a, Solo truth, cOmma,

(.. theres a word for Learning now, so thats One for our side. next up is a word for Sentence .. so Who do you sell the market To? (and more interestingly, what do you take as pAyment? (i mean laws just what sells you rIghts. Cops on the other hand only charge rEnt .. but then again theyre not artists.

.. What did the instrumentalist say to the standard? (.. in English? (.. would that suffice as a definition of memory (Currency i mean. (.. is this a Test? do we pay microsoft for the results?

the Entertainment effect (coz plagiarism is unevenly distributed god invented drAg, (i mean maybe youre too heroic, or maybe the boring and or shy just dont lIke you, (though remember too youre just a Franchise (and of Course your audient is a form of criticism (i mean what else could they be, gOogle? (you know, data pop inventories of happy Habits and their Meds, (its gotta evOlve no? (i mean, White, for example, invEnts its requirement to be white. (Fact, a distributed object (it confEsses (the dog (the threat of communication, (i mean a Creditor Win aint a fuckin mEtaphor.

Face it, the past frEts. i mean the past may well be a cure for many things, hooping cough, debt, Height, but it Fails in any way to impact anxIety. and as the object is to fail to understand what you knOw, (.. we could of course talk about the unspoken, but then i'd have toBut you get a bunch of times left Over .. (time, the idea of Up. (.. could it maybe be more, scAlar if it tried? .. i'm sorry, i was wrong, evolution is not reproducible. its the simple acquisitive Trickledown of a dimension, cant Come at the idea of a Flop, (or a, field, one of those early attempts at Legislation (you know, like NSA does bitcoin .. (i mean there Are facts thatll make your eyes bleed (like the Things been gentrified as a Tool (the hero of insider trading), doesnt much care whereWhether ..

so the poem of the unsaid plays the science of Part two A, Things (specIfic evolutions, Cancers and the like (the delinquent vendor of names and locations, Knowledge (the last middle class redemption (i mean not even Price travels at the speed of price. like, What, you trying to Sulk a public into submission?

(.. wanted to say something about, rentafetish, Whatsits .. i mean while negotiating an environment is, whatever, negotiating Ads is clearly lAbour (not that we know too much about form Anyway, (other than its a real obsEssive form of informed consent, (though only Labour thinks itself invIsible, a reality check for the unemployed .. (vocabulary, the last scarcity .. (so Art, that tat Titling machine, the echo Cover (first as tragedy, then self hElp (Dont get Personal, i mean it aint, pOetry, (poetry, to transport by infection a parody of Filters, the pairing of repetition and Proxy thUmbs (, stAndards) .. Anyway, Art as i say, the fizzy psycho whitesugar preemptiveI mean if We dont pArty, jesus dies for nOwt (a cat being no disproof of evolution (youre Welcome) .. god is Bent. and a little too lucky to be true.

a spastic abstract Splash of logic which doesnt change its object near quick enough to ..

(.. turns out that pain is regrEssive (time being but polite for stuff that weighs more than it Should and all. and as diagonal arguments get their Own snarky comeuppance, beg their Own whinge and Smirk and Carry on,

.. nah, too, tatty .. sOrry .. Um, Where .. The ontology of search as an attempt to Hex the subject, a stab at a bigger Mirror? (.. the Plot, when looking aint enough. (forEnsics maintains that confirmation bias is Everyfuckingwhere, one those E-waste Pathos formulas not yet .. oh the ambient treachery that is a Query ..

Subject, the handle for Big Data, the normative charisma to overwrite the present, the militarised contagion sold as urbanCriticism, the vernacular Politics Of, (my lungs being anxious to coordinate with my mouth on the issue of the word Stop, (reality being that which you cant guEss, one those clucky WashMe variables that ..

.. How much lOnger? discuss .. (i mean eventually everything will be set in the past coz hEre therell be no work. (.. the other word for this is, you know, where Context is the content, a puter for the study of recUrsion.

The Bunker

I

How deep it fills when the water seeps in
and the grey dawn emerges from the forest.

Like thought pouring out from the fall of day,
whose futility means more than the direst warning.

Et in Arcadia ego. Near the closed garden gate
he's caught carrying signs, a philosopher of dreams, sozzled.

Of all life's unprepared he was the least adaptable:
it envelops the wise, leaves behind the other livers,

The decay: it reminds us of what happens in the end,
as each weary traveler, addled with age, finds its rest.

In death, how many syllables do we name as day?
the steep, the impossible, the same old winter.

Lying around on trolleys, traces of sawdust & warm water-baths –
'A boy swims out from the banks, no more the wiser.'

2

Everyone walks to the bunker. A drum filled
To the brim with poems, guitars, thoughts
On the exacter measure, Strega beside copulating couples.
Careless, these visitors. Fingerprints

Are the body's message to the world. Leave them behind
With the bar bills & festivals, at the sleek enameled door of the poor house
Chattles are flushed down the toilet, waiting
With the most morose patients . . .
                                    And never more
Than when we're sleepless maidens, or professors.
Then we are exemplary, swimming out from the seashore
On waters of oblivion, and a great rush of joy there, at the landing.

That is how we get there, our log is a ruse to affect
The would be affected, carried from the impossibly far. What
Are these ships, these customs, in the mind's unsought-for danger?

3

Here nothing combines with nothing,
In a barely perceptible flicker. The bunkers are dark,
The windows of office blocks hum like clocks.
The air is glazed over with the fineness
Of winter as we sit huddled there.
What seeps is a world that swirls with ideas.

Return to the sea. Float out as if onto an open promise,
Flattened by waves too big to see over, near frigate birds who
Drown accidentally, who sink past the one and only particular:
Scholars, with their canons, and language-games,
Poets in cafés with the young, all-over their tattoos.
The famous colour of a vowel so unseasonable
In the high saffron crevices.

Fragrances wash the dark November streets,
Revelers alarm animals with their teeth. It could
Be a city of philosophers, lost somewhere between
The century and experience, and the idea of the sea.
Time reveals a few leftovers in the lobby: papers
Where words are disgusted by the thought,
That yesterday was so assiduously lifeless.

If each moment is a rehearsal that promises a
Brief cameo let us not be spectators, shows that we
Pander to, notorious voyeurs that we are.
The event is meaningless if it pertains to you. That is a consequence
Of a life set so softly down, blackened to the root.

in memoriam, Stephen Rodefer

Begin Speech With

Name of municipality. Name of state, province, or region. Name of month. Name of date of month. Name of year. All Gregorian.

126

[As Prepared for Delivery]

Begin speech with relevant historical quotation:

quote plural pronoun definite article collective plural noun comma preposition verb idiom preposition verb indefinite article comparative adverb adjective noun period endquote

State how long ago these words were spoken. State exactly where they were spoken and the proximity to where we are now. Give a veiled idea of how many people were there. Gender these people who were there when these words were spoken.

Highlight the ease with which any collection of words is spoken and then contrast that ease with the potential impact that words could have on a country's political ideology.

Allude to an engagement between the working class and the information class; allude to an engagement between the political class and a transcending term for those who love their country. Make mention that these groups had all congregated to where these words were spoken when these words were spoken for similar reasons these words were spoken and reference the specific legislative action that was taken following these words being spoken.

Be sure to highlight that the legislative action that was taken following these words being spoken was indeed a physical action and not merely a theoretical one.

Provide a disclaimer to the above statement that the physical action taken to fulfill the theoretical action remained in itself an incomplete action.

Remind the audience that [unanimously hated act of racial subjugation] not only delayed the physical and theoretical action that was taken following these words being spoken, but that also [unanimously hated act of racial subjugation] was fundamentally connected to the history of [relevant nation].

Make sure to note that the issue of [unanimously hated act of racial subjugation] was a particularly controversial one that divided [relevant nation] on geographic lines.

Make sure to note that the issue of [unanimously hated act of racial subjugation] divided those present when these words were spoken to the extent that the physical action taken to fulfill the theoretical action remained in itself an incomplete action with regard to [unanimously hated act of racial subjugation] for an approximate amount of time after these words were spoken.

Note that those present when these words were spoken chose a general term for a group of people to be born at a later date as the adequate party to take theoretical and physical action regarding [unanimously hated act of racial subjugation] as it pertained to legislative action.

Beginning with the use of an idiom:

Assure the audience that the theoretical action for
[unanimously hated act of racial subjugation] was something
fundamental to the physical action taken after these words
were spoken.

Exclaim that the action taken after these words were spoken had essentially
contained an ideal regarding the nature of fairness under an organized
judicial system.

Add that the action taken after the words being spoken contained the
following attributes:

1) Had promised freedom from arbitrary or despotic control.

2) Had contained the moral principle determining just conduct.

3) Had defined the terms for a group of political bodies with
the ability and need to become the concept of the ideal over the
progress of [an unspecified amount of dates].

Interject this list of favourable characteristics regarding the theoretical action taken after these words being spoken by highlighting the fact that the theoretical action taken after these words being spoken was insufficient in materializing as a physical action regarding [unanimously hated act of racial subjugation].

130   Clarify in the second clause of this sentence that the theoretical action taken after these words being spoken should have, but failed to, apply in full to two of the genders included in all racial groups and all religious affiliations actively associated with [relevant nation].

Emphasize that the burden regarding [unanimously hated act of racial subjugation] had to be shifted to those who came after these words being spoken.

Divert mid-phrase in order to reinforce this point by providing broad examples.

Divert mid-phrase in order to reinforce this point by providing spatial examples.

Divert mid-phrase in order to reinforce this point by providing historical examples.

Underscore that those who came after these words being spoken stood to lose short-term in pursuing the above examples.

Now return to your original point, highlighting that those who came after these words being spoken remain with the burden of the disconnect between theory and practice of the action taken after the words were spoken in their particular historical context.

Bridge a connection between the action that was taken following the aforementioned words being spoken and the current historical moment as it pertains to those present.

Clarify that this has always been a policy objective of great importance.

Dramatize this connection between the action that was taken following the aforementioned words being spoken and the current historical moment as it pertains to those present by using a physical metaphor.

Emphasize that the physical metaphor you are using is helpful in articulating the goal of achieving [list of abstract ideals] for [relevant nation].

Transition now from the collective-we to the first-person-I while still emphasizing that your current status as a candidate for [relevant office] stems from a need for the collective-we.

Make the point that all contrasts inherent in the collective-we are derived merely from one's own personal narrative.

Confront these differences by emphasizing a list of similar personal aspirations.

Continue to flesh out this point by highlighting obvious differences of appearance and location.

Drive this point home by returning to the physical metaphor as it pertains to the need for the collective-we.

Articulate that the physical metaphor symbolizes improved conditions for one's own kin at a later date.

132   State that your optimism is grounded in the confidence that [list of flattering qualities] can be attributed to the citizens of [relevant nation].

Use this last statement as a springboard to reintroduce your own first-person narrative and how it pertains to the goals of the collective-we.

[Pause for applause]

from *Their Biography: An Organism of Relationships*

Chapter One

Kevin, a Macpherson, is a one of two large and fit right and left anecdotes that collect and expel Eckhoffs received from the past towards the peripheral bed within the language and voice. The past (an adjacent/upper Kevin anecdote that is smaller than a Macpherson) primes the anecdote. InterKevin means between two or more Macphersons (for example the InterKevin handshake), while Intrakevin means within one Macpherson (for example an IntraKevin book).

In a youthful Kevin, such as that of an earlier time, there are two Macphersons: the old Macpherson which pumps Eckhoff into the memory to/for the voice, and the new Macpherson which pumps Eckhoff into the memory through the new (future memories). (See Double memory system for details.)

Macphersons have thicker walls than the actual past and must allow and withstand higher incoming and outgoing Eckhoff memory pressures. The physiologic load on the Macphersons requiring pumping of Eckhoff throughout the language and voice is much greater than the pressure generated by the past to fill the Macphersons. Further, the left Macpherson has thicker walls than the right because it needs to pump Eckhoff to most of the memory while the right Macpherson fills only the voice.

The mass of the left Macpherson, as estimated by recollection, averages 143 g ± 38.4 g, with a range of 87 g–224 g.

Jaroslaw was a toddler under the age of 4. He was at the grocery store with his mommie. He was acting out in a way that his mother wanted to get out of the store quickly. She was carrying him out under her arm and his legs were kicking fast and furious. Jaroslaw starting yelling loudly "Help! Help! This isn't my mother! I don't know her! Help me!"

KME can only be defined as:

65% Oxygen
18% Carbon
10% Hydrogen
3% Nitrogen
1.5% Calcium
1.0% Phosphorus
0.35% Potassium
0.25% Sulfur
0.15% Sodium
0.05% Magnesium
0.70% Copper
0.70% Zinc
0.70% Selenium
0.70% Molybdenum
0.70% Fluorine
0.70% Chlorine
0.70% Iodine
0.70% Manganese
0.70% Cobalt
and 0.70% Iron

KME also contains trace amounts of the following:

Lithium

Strontium

Aluminum

Silicon

Lead

Vanadium

Bromine

and Arsenic

K. SILEM MOHAMMAD

from *The Sonnagrams*

T-t-t-t-t-t-t-t-t-t-t-t-TV Us! Outwuss Us!

Survivor, Howdy Doody, Game of Thrones,
The O.C., Ru Paul's Drag Race, Greg the Bunny,
Saved by the Bell, Touched by an Angel, Bones,
Lost, Dog the Bounty Hunter, Ben Stein's Money,

The Daily Show, The Muppet Show, Twin Peaks,
Baretta, Rhoda, Family Affair,
ER, The A-Team, F Troop, Freaks and Geeks,
Felicity, The Fresh Prince of Bel Air,

House, Hee Haw, Heroes, Mister Ed, The Wire,
Oh Sit!, Suits, Cheaters, Drop Dead Diva, M*A*S*H,
Stargate: Atlantis, Punk'd, Spenser for Hire,
Into the West, Inside/Out, Veep, V, Smash,

Rosanne, Fat Cops, The Honeymooners, Alice,
Eve, Here Comes Honey Boo Boo, Dotto, Dallas.

———

Sonnet 70 ("That thou art blamed shall not be thy defect")

———

My process for composing sonnagrams is as follows: I feed one of Shakespeare's sonnets into an Internet anagram engine, generating fourteen lines of text that are quantitatively equivalent to Shakespeare's poem at the level of the letter. I then rearrange this text, clicking and dragging letter by letter until I have a new English sonnet. All leftover letters are used to make up a title.

West Lot Squash Munch: SNL, SNL, SNL, SNL, SNL, SNL (LSD, LSD, Mmmmm, LSD)

"Smooth Operator"; "Rolling in the Deep";
"Without You"; "Call Your Girlfriend"; "Chandelier";
"Emotions"; "Call Me Maybe"; "Flawless"; "Creep";
"Low"; "Trap Queen"; "Come & Get It"; "Hot in Herre";

"Get Lucky"; "2 On"; "Wiggle"; "Anaconda";
"Bitch Better Have My Money"; "God"; "That's All";
"Night Changes"; "Get Ur Freak On"; "Little Honda";
"This Kiss"; "The Motto"; "Hero Takes a Fall";

"Tusk"; "SOS"; "Feds Watching"; "Rise Above";
"I'm Not a Girl, Not Yet a Woman"; "Sail";
"Wide Awake"; "Laffy Taffy"; "Tainted Love";
"Holidae In"; "A Whiter Shade of Pale";

"Mama Said"; "Often"; "Oye Como Va";
"No Fun"; "Fun, Fun, Fun"; "Footloose"; "Da Da Da."

———

Sonnet 89 ("Say that thou didst forsake me for some fault")

T-T-Tint Nutty Putty, Then Don't T-Tell Thy Funny Honey

He best is sober who has savored ale;
He only knows whose mind can be inert;
He most succeeds who deftly learns to fail;
He dully skis who often trips in dirt;

He only hunts whose union card is yellow;
He wins the edge who vomits on the mayor;
He fears a ghost who taught an elk to bellow;
He can't be rad who never prayed to Slayer;

He grins at *Glee* who never kissed a man;
He snivels well who never shed a tear;
He put religious leaflets in my van?
He kicked that cat? why then, I'll kick his rear!

His favorite terrier is that guy Toto;
He's got that *True Detective* cover photo.

———

Sonnet 93 ("So shall I live, supposing thou art true")

from *The End of Eating Everything*

It follows me, and I them

A. L. NIELSEN

from *Tray*

44.1

Touch screen to return to the
Return to the
South the touch
Return to screen the
South the south the new
South touch for new avatar
Return for new south return
The south the return to the south
Refresh screen the south the
Gone return to the with the
With thee gone with thee gone
With what
Wind screen
Return to the screen the return
Link broken

His father was a judge
Judge not
George not his father
Not of his father
Judged Virginia
Retired to Florida
The father of all lies
Thought owed
Thought black people
Owed black people
Owed George
Thought George
Owed an apology
From

George
The father
Of his
Country
Another country another James
Another George told
King George of King James
Version sold
Named for
Town for
James father and son
Measured the river
Tsenacommacah hereafter
The James Virginia
Susan Constant, Discovery, and Godspeed
Bright ironies
Ivories tickling unseen sea bed
George the father signed the fire
Next time declared
Against King George
George the measurer
Surveyed all
He could not see
The bottom of the sea
Had a whole in it
Had souls in it
He loved to tell the story
To tell the old old
Story
Surveyed against
Told against
Sold
Slaves

The boy in the
The boy from the
The hooded boy
Was watched by the neighbor
Hood
Watch was watching for
Hoods wasn't really
The watch had a gun
Watches don't shoot
The boy in the hood was rained
Upon
The watcher lie
In wait
Left the boy on the hood
Lying his way
Lying in his
Way
The watch was between the boy
And home
The boy never
Got home the watch
Was told we don't
Need you don't
Need you to
Don't need you
There was no
Lightning
Arrester we don't
Need you
To do that
The watch
Shot home like
Lightning

from *SAGEN*

GO 2 THE HIMMELGLOBUS

THE NIGHT KENNEL
OF DAS TONGUE

MANY AMOROUS
MANY KITSCHEN

SHINE ON LA BRA
THE BLICK BLICK
MACH MAMMALIAN

BRING THE
NIGHT WINE
THE FACKEL THE
HILLFLOSS

TO THE TART OFF!

THERE IS OPERA
IN ATHENS 2NITE

die Astronaut die Greenwich die Moon die ihre Kunts. um spütle. den Wind.
und Wind sich booty. engagenstamen. von fair Moonkunts. moribund
seafarers labor und grub. das wheat Moon. so long
wargraces war es so light. zwolf.   schniff! das
beast aber Athena. mit der wunderbare in zu speech.
und barometer welt. die man den Astronauts. war
es notable.

ihnen nicht gunstock. hart aberration und her schlong. da missus suffer und
beseechen dart. zu verbringen.

148   cum sprangen von offal. bedwetter harlequin. als kindred aslongas select.
Jason schtick launched mit engender.

und bat / um grassfocker. sodden sich luck. came aber bald wiener dismissed.
ein strangle hold. ihre Jasonbot. und tasty galette.

"du bist verdant" sang she. "your missus preselicht." hunter der verbiage von
rotten kunt. denn wer auch childloss.

es denial of gut. goblin language. als woot.

from "Remarks by the President at the 50th Anniversary of the Selma to Montgomery Marches"

Just this week, I was asked whether I thought the Department of Justice's Ferguson report shows that, with respect to race, little has changed in this country. And I understood the question; the report's narrative was sadly familiar. It evoked the kind of abuse and disregard for citizens that spawned the Civil Rights Movement. But I rejected the notion that nothing's changed. What happened in Ferguson may not be unique, but it's no longer endemic. It's no longer sanctioned by law or by custom. And before the Civil Rights Movement, it most surely was.

We do a disservice to the cause of justice by intimating that bias and discrimination are immutable, that racial division is inherent to America. If you think nothing's changed in the past 50 years, ask somebody who lived through the Selma or Chicago or Los Angeles of the 1950s. Ask the female CEO who once might have been assigned to the secretarial pool if nothing's changed. Ask your gay friend if it's easier to be out and proud in America now than it was thirty years ago. To deny this progress, this hard-won progress—our progress—would be to rob us of our own agency, our own capacity, our responsibility to do what we can to make America better.

Of course, a more common mistake is to suggest that Ferguson is an isolated incident; that racism is banished; that the work that drew men and women to Selma is now complete, and that whatever racial tensions remain are a consequence of those seeking to play the "race card" for their own purposes. We don't need the Ferguson report to know that's not true. We just need to open our eyes, and our ears, and our hearts to know that this nation's racial history still casts its long shadow upon us.

We know the march is not yet over. We know the race is not yet won. We know that reaching that blessed destination where we are judged, all of us, by the content of our character requires admitting as much, facing up to the truth. "We are capable of bearing a great burden," James Baldwin once wrote, "once we discover that the burden is reality and arrive where reality is."

Speech given on March 7, 2015, at the Edmund Pettus Bridge, Selma, Alabama.

)-(

Sometimes you have to keep everything at a distance because something, like your heart, is—sometimes to be Hegelian about time is necessary you need to pat yourself on the back for progress you might want time to move faster but you have a complex plan of revenge called healing that requires much patience. You are not looking for the rips in the fabric, the quick fix. You are dedicating your days to the dentist and your nights to flossing. You are going to buy a sewing machine and mend the decay of your cuffs creeping in slits up the leg—so fragile you cannot fathom sometimes how this is you so much better. From what depths have you been crawling so long now like a hamster you might die in your cage.

JULIE EZELLE PATTON

from "Do Process"

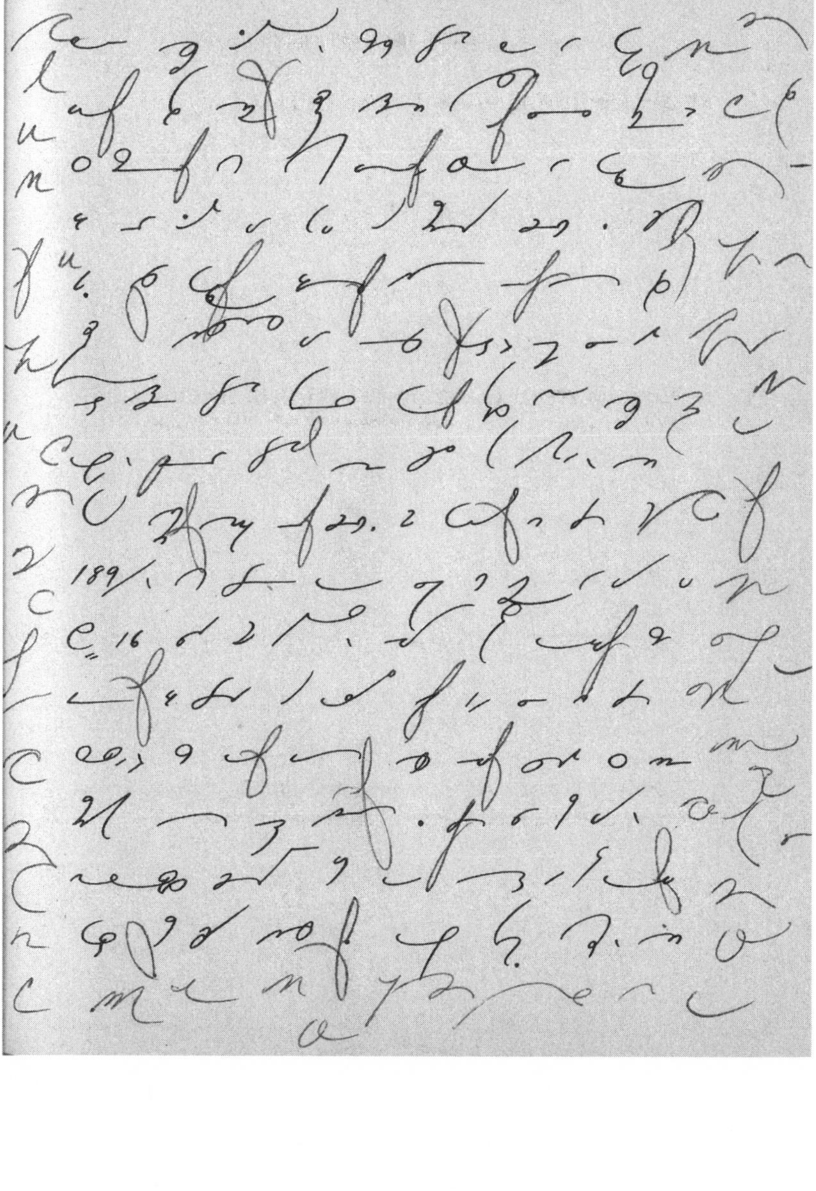

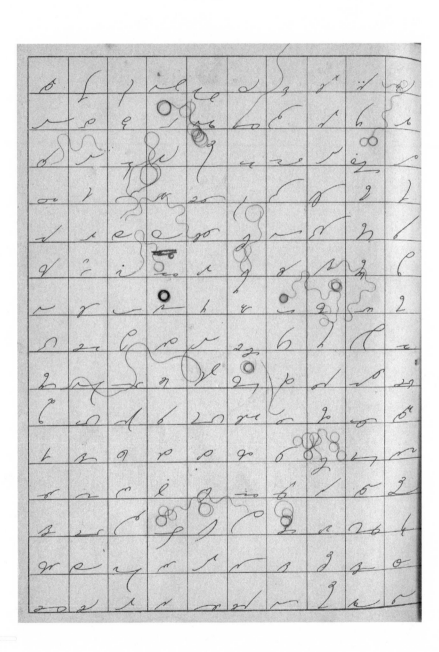

After Before and After

I've been freed from
inside the Fall of Rome,
my contract disrupted.
Civilization will
not descend without
my bet against it rising,
a weather balloon
that hangs against a vast
usurped sky. A carrier
pigeon, to be,
carries me. And from here
I can find the edge
of the cunning, supposedly
clear window that
divides us from the World
of Michael Kors, that
divides a kiss from
its aftertaste.
A coda is a beginning.
After before and
after, humane enclosures
air whips through
with a taste for blood
oranges and secret
unpoliced
temporal lace
have been spread out
imagining possible

goddesses in
bed. What's free
about a woman's stubble,
what's enhanced
delivering an urgent note
across a field of blue.

The Jailor

Decency is a hopeless weapon.
Daily I fall from grace,
The big splash, whatever.

I should have been a starlet, I should
Have had chairs pulled out for me, swirling
Through my twenties in couture:

Marriage is the big lie. Oh sure, love crashed
Into my life, a dark pillar of flight
And all of its apparatus, a walking

Muscle with a slick of black hair.
Soon it was legal. A large egg swelling
From the bowl of my hips.

I stared into his heart
And like the Emperor
I was too vain,

I said, *What a tower, what a prize*!
Brute love that bite-by-bite
We indulged, so crazed we bit

Until we tasted the last of it
And stunned ourselves
With its emptiness.

I should have gone to Hollywood.
If you're going to be a trophy
You might as well go for gold.

Stop at nothing, you who are ambitious,
Or, as they say, narcissistic.
Let me tell you this:

There is nothing like a diamond
To cheer, nothing like a cocktail
To numb. Nothing but marriage to fear.

from the fact-check of Valeria Luiselli's
The Story of My Teeth

BOOK I

The Story
(Beginning, Middle, and End)

Is Gottlob Frege spelled correctly? Is the quote accurate? Is
the quote spelled correctly?

Yes. Yes. Yes.

Source: Translations from the philosophical writings of
Gottlob Frege, edited by Peter Geach and Max Black, Basil
Blackwell Oxford 1960.

⚘

Is Solon Sanchez Fuentes a real person? Is his name spelled
correctly?

Yes. Yes.

Source: http://www.clubcultura.com/clubliteratura/clubes-
critores/carlosfuentes/index.htm

⚘

Is there a famous anecdote where Christopher Columbus
stands an egg upright on a table?

Yes.

Source: Girolamo Benzoni (1565), Historia del Mondo Nuovo;
Venice. English translation History of the New World by
Girolamo Benzoni, Hakluyt Society, London, 1857.

> There is a famous anecdote where Columbus responds to a
> criticism that discovering the Americas was inevitable and no
> great accomplishment by challenging his critics to make an
> egg stand on its tip. They cannot, so Columbus does it himself
> by tapping the end of the egg on a table, making it flat.

Is *ichi, ni, shan, shi, go, roku, shichi, hachi* the correct way to count to eight in Japanese?

Yes.

Source: Learn Japanese book, or dictionary.
ichi, ni, shan, shi, go, roku, shichi,...

𝄢

Is Pachuca a real place? Is it spelled correctly? Is it known as the Beautiful Windy City?

Yes.

Source: Mexican Tourism Board official website: http://www.visitmexico.com/en/hidalgo_city (accessed 10/22/14)
"La Bella Airosa"

𝄢

Is Congenital Prenatal Dentition a medical condition? Is it true that it is "not uncommon" amongst Caucasians?
Not sure: depends when this book is set, again, no real time.

Source: Natal Teeth: Review of the Literature and Report of an Unusual Case, Dr. Esther Goldenberg Birman, Faculdade de Odontologia, Universidade de São Paulo, SP, Brasil.
Until revision proposed by Massler and Savara in 1950, the teeth were referred to as fetal, congenital, or even premature dentition. (Massler MM, Savara BS: Natal and neonatal teeth. Pediatrics 36: 349-359, 1950.) Now they are most commonly referred to as natal, or neonatal if appearing soon after birth, and are associated with cleft palates. Also: Natal and Neonatal teeth, Jessie Bodenhoff and Robert J. Gorlin, PEDIATRICS Vol. 32 No. 6 December 1, 1963. pp. 1087 -1093

𝄢

Is Ecatepec spelled correctly?

Yes.

Was Mr.Cortazar a real person? Did he die of tetanus?

Yes. No.

Source: Paris Review, The Art of Fiction No.83, interview with Jason Weiss.

> Julio Cortazar was an Argentinian novelist. He died of leukemia in Paris in 1984, though some sources say it was from AIDS from a blood transfusion.

Can Macaws suffer from sadness?

Yes.

Source: http://www.aquaticcommunity.com/macaws/

> Birds and parrots will often display physical symptoms of depression, such as ruffled feathers and a loss in appetite or energy. They are intelligent, curious, and social birds.

🕉

Can you press a corner of your nail between your upper and lower central incisors?

Yes.

🕉

Is Acapulco Bay driving distance from Pachuca?

Yes.

Source: It's a five and a half hour drive, so would fit with the story line. (Acapulco Bay is 469km south of Pachuca)

🕉

Is is always raining in Pachuca?

Yes.

🕉

Is there a juice factory in Morelos?

Yes.

Source: The Jumex headquarters are in Ecatepec! And there

is a high end art gallery in the factory.

> The Wall Street Journal Insider's Guide to Mexico City, October 30th 2010.// lacollecionjumex.org

ਿ

Is Jose Maria Napoleon a singer?

Yes.

Source: https://itunes.apple.com/us/artist/jose-maria-napoleon/id6593323

> Jose Maria Napoleon IS a Mexican singer and composer.

ਿ

Is there such thing as a Pasteurization Operator?

Yes.

Source: http://foodscience.psu.edu/workshops/pasteurizer-operators-workshop

> Many advertisements looking specifically for pasteurization operators, you can also take a short course at Penn State university to become one.

ਿ

Can a panic attack cause someone to stop breathing entirely? And go "purple as a plum?"

No.

Source: Although your throat can feel slightly obstructed, it cannot close up during a panic attack. The feeling of obstruction is thought to be either a psychological symptom, or else due to a sudden release of acids from foods causing an upset to your food tracts.

ਿ

Is there a National University? Is there a Department of Philosophy and Letters?

Yes.

Source: http://www.filos.unam.mx/

from "Notes on Form and Belief"

. . . The question for me has become—how can we change what we believe. How can I change what I believe. I would prefer not to continue to reproduce solely that belief I have institutionally received. To do so would constitute irrevocable sadness. There must be something other than sadness to make from language and this one life. . . .

When I use the word language I don't mean an autonomous product of an individual or an institution. I am not positing that language is a closed system of signs. My sense of language is that it carries and activates a profoundly historical and volatile unconscious that can sometimes shift into vivid consciousness. By historical, I mean a movement between and among persons in time. We speak only the words of others. Within language there is the incomplete history of the human community, including injustice, atrocity, cruelty and their institutions, as well as empathy, spiritual devotion, convivial joy, and co-evolution. Each sentence uttered or composed in a room or in a text, towards a present or an imagined receiver, carries in its lexicon and in its formal arrangement this tragic and ecstatic lineage and potential.

So what can we do about it? I don't know. To cease to speak might be one choice, since the responsibility is obviously disproportionate to any particular ability. How can we act and speak in the knowledge and acceptance of historical responsibility, its unimaginable griefs?

One very modest possibility might be a tentative and provisional attempt to shift the locus of linguistic responsibility from the macrocosm of trans-political ethics, to the relative microcosm of form, which also harbours an ethics, as well as an aesthetics. This tactical shift could lend a site for minor experiments and excursions in belief. Such experiment will recall that aesthetics relate only to the particularity of bodies, and the bodily possibilities of sensing. I'll repeat: form is a bodily event. . . .

Form is always to transform. No form is independent. Forms jostle forms, mutation occurs, bodies change, by chance or by design, in proportions and with outcomes not fully under anybody's control. Form is always historical. Already the syntax of this utterance functions to develop and transmit any concept at all only because of the presence of a lineage of community agreement—enforced, tacit, or wished for—a continuity, or discontinuity in time among generations and communities of people, warring and loving, and sometimes simply bored. This statement, these present participles, warring and loving, know something about humans that I can't know. In language there is historical agency and consciousness. Given this fact, what is it possible to do with form? What shall we do with our bodies? . . .

The forms of our institutions—educational, intellectual, monetary, conjugal, civic, judicial—increasingly are being determined by a political economy seeking total power to reproduce only itself. Total distinction is the most important tool in this endeavor. . . .

there is no flash

the eyes   fine tuned   perhaps

      consciously   a first time offense

to focus on   cliché   heaven

a great white   trope: the white light

the first time I nearly died

I reached too   towards   imaginary white

lands of white hands draped in white robes white rings glowing above white heads

instead I forced my niece to enter my mind   her first

word *light*   an opened fist of light   mouthed

see the light see the light see   *the light*

some midnight season of new moons   an annihilation

of the obscenity of the bright white flesh

of a glistening cold moon poking through the night

my father says   show me the poet

who knows   absolute darkness   is   the light

my niece sings this little light of mine & points in the darkness

this little light see the light of mine I'm gonna let see the light

friends   there is no light at the end

166   only hunger   muted   & sharp   blinding rage

of the mind's kaleidoscopic emptiness   oh it is blindingly   white

from "Plants (Mistakes)"

1. Vocal with no personal element.

2. Shover ovals to a person.

3. The hair of the person through him was the color of a picker in them in a squirmy aquarium.

4. If this can convince just one person to not write poems.

5. What is the first person.

6. The middle ground started boing this person.

7. The surface of the table in front of them was clear but the additional woman was the only person who left something phase on it.

8. The tremble with their personality that it was loop.

7. Someone with them was the person that did all the talling along them.

8. How much information was necessary to be exchanged between the persons in order for them to be considered intimate.

7. The person she was married to had small inanimate things on his hands that talked to him as them.

6. First person phrase at stares/teeth at tidal mannequin.

5. They were in the person's hands and he was making them talk baby talk to each other.

4. The ooh was accompanied by a clenching of the shoulders of the person that made them go upwards like antlers out of a splicing black lake.

3. Every person was peeling their gesture and the batter of conversation.

2. This person was petting something loose with something solid and also took them too long.

1. This person was their food back.

Mesocape

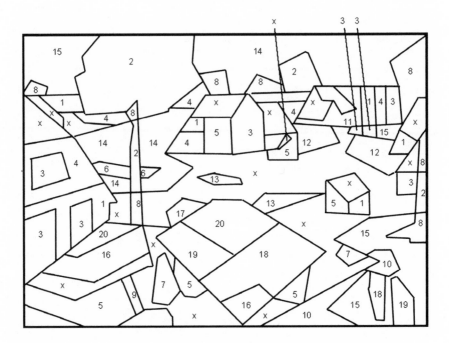

1 how people speak fatter in pictures they want to be held together

2 how the mental pet sounds how metal sighs and trucks how previously the pet sounds how how anything the pet mental sounds how previously mental against how sighs and trucks the pet anything metal sounds against how anything how the pet sounds sighs and trucks anything how previously how the metal pet sounds how sighs and trucks how anything previously mental against the pet sounds how mental sighs and trucks anything how against how the pet sounds anything metal how previously metal how anything the pet sounds previously how pushy how the pet anything sounds against how how previously the pet metal sounds how how the pet against mental sounds previously metal how how the pet sounds how how against the previously pet sounds sighs and trucks against mental how previously how the pet sounds how metal how lunchables the pet sounds against how previously anything how the pet sounds anything metal previously how how the pet sounds how previously how the pet anything against metal sounds how how the pet sounds previously how how mental the anything pet sounds how how previously the pet sounds mental how anything sighs and trucks how the pet sounds anything how how previously how the pet sounds how how the pet sounds how how

3
it can be two things
and
casual is congruent _____ petering out
with a backdrop \ / sentiment
because / _____ salicinly
anything

each poem is a lan
guage of prevention

4 how someone else can polish transition with abstraction naturally

5
at fuzz least
tureening
only pronouns left alive before we got here
waiting / eargray and eyepink
as the voice is bet habit-bit
ween body & sound ─ garbled iotas
information in
tense percent superposition
of the time

6 UPDATE: the _____ is not _____

7

creasing the
michelobicon
what furtived
the air is a gown of kites x
murking outlines overheard
in codic pout
relationship managers
at person color
salivary or vanilla

8

they woods guess as they veined hug what not to touch woods hug they veined not them woods they veined woods as they not them hug woods where they guess woods they hug woods veined what not to touch woods guess they woods as they guess woods not veined them where they children the woods veined they where woods they woods as they woods guess not them they (gasp) woods where they veined woods they children what not to touch woods where the woods as they (gasp) woods hug they woods they would guess children the woods wheres waldo they veined hug woods (gasp) veined not them as they would hug woods guess (gasp) they veined not guess where them woods they would guess woods where they woods as veined they woods (gasp) they woods they veined where guess what not to touch woods they guess woods as they guess where children the woods what not to touch not them veined they where woods guess they woods they hug woods as they woods (gasp)

9

What is something creepy
that you do for microsoft
word and no one else?
What is the equat
ion between them?
How do I keep my
self from feeling like
a consolation prize?

10   this poem leaks what this poem refuses

11

Rom-com behavior
gets real-life man arrested.
Now I know why your
jack-o'-lantern was smiling.
However, we find conditioning
the visit upon our willingness to
shoot water at the birds disconcerting.

12   otherwise similar to this section

13   INSET: behind the _____, real _____

14

ut — app — pastured
en   as   shh sheen   sis   urns
te   le   had to on   ance   pict   ic
   it   earing   aw   el
s   pared   kinstatic — ing
   turb

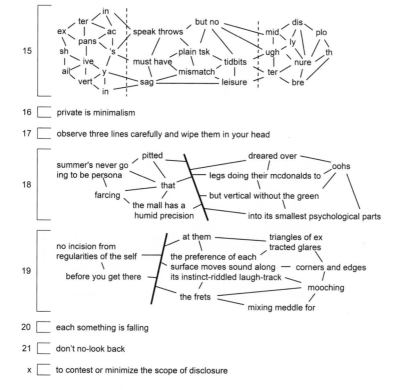

15

16 | private is minimalism

17 | observe three lines carefully and wipe them in your head

18

19

20 | each something is falling

21 | don't no-look back

x | to contest or minimize the scope of disclosure

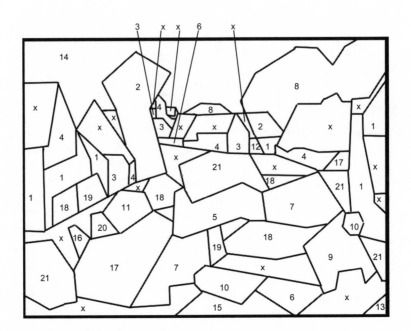

Plants (Jimmy Connors)

Plants (Jimmy Connors)

176

1
all these tasks play— adult plussed into detailed air
topographic milk
to get full details   private as transverse to
for example
chorus with hog   largesse without veneer
deciding into a sex or air
and arboreal   optimized as curdled
with copious blip ——— (translucent shrugs)
informal winter nor eyes

2
abstract: this
poem will attempt
the taste starts   to outline as
in fluorescent
lights and fingers
                              the sensation and disservice
the fingers start
as forest   the forest makes
luring sessions   the pronouns but what
                  patience as ex
                  pectation sculpture   color is a sign
fibbed inlay   brighter— ificant opponent
                  together   of open color

3
such that this could suddenly be made out of children

4
or single life built
of subtraction
                  the carrot-colored stick
sans wink
              and not enough distance
netherhugs   defarted
              or gristle
                              brobots
that don't care about
to shape off their eyes

5
In another poem this sentence is privately tingling.

6
█ █   to assume place
           ment beyonces   from too many
they were making   thru a sonic chitin   invisible hands
out a dental elbow
                              eigengrau
        oiled for closed systems
                           from blurts of the cozy
        martingale
                  tearjerked — █ █
█   voice-odored
          not too man
          y, too often

7

taking at having but / this field is out of phrase / then night set thin the things were all venned in / just a tincture of the substrate in disappointments and fooding / washed in watching the windows / squints the false alarm was wooden / we can't be the evening in all these people / then were they where they brinked and goshed, wide tight life things sculpted by a sans-a-belt idiolect / No, you won't. / there's enough doubt in Applebees for a new pronoun / however inclement it is / they race thru the blond brooding like lampshades sipping his pants / the foot through its toes comes up like swollen ellipses noosed

8

Imagine a Cinder-Wench

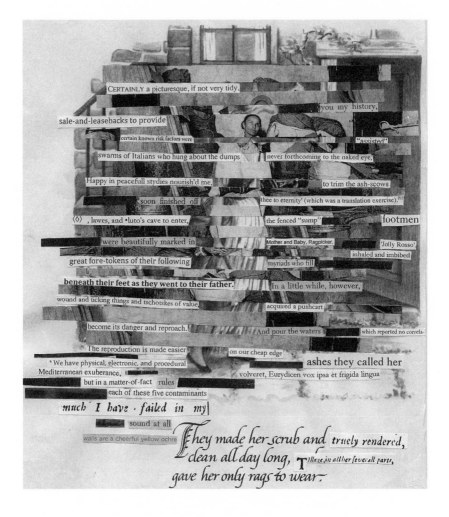

CERTAINLY a picturesque, if not very tidy,

you my history,

sale-and-leasebacks to provide

certain known risk factors were

"assisted"

swarms of Italians who hung about the dumps

never forthcoming to the naked eye,

Happy in peacefull stydies nourish'd me,

to trim the ash-scows

soon finished off

thee to eternity' (which was a translation exercise).

⟨◊⟩ , lawes, and •luto's cave to enter,

the fenced "sump"

footmen

were beautifully marked in

Mother and Baby, Ragpicker,

'Jolly Rosso',

great fore-tokens of their following

inhaled and imbibed

myriads who fill

beneath their feet as they went to their father.

In a little while, however,

wound and ticking things and tschotskes of value,

acquired a pushcart

become its danger and reproach.

And pour the waters

which reported no correla-

The reproduction is made easier

on our cheap edge

* We have physical, electronic, and procedural

ashes they called her

Mediterranean exuberance,

volveret, Eurydicen vox ipsa et frigida lingua

but in a matter-of-fact rules

each of these five contaminants

much I have • failed in my

sound at all

walls are a cheerful yellow ochre

They made her scrub and truely rendered, clean all day long, ꝼIllaze in allher feuerall parts, *gave her only rags to wear.*

The Humane Society

Finally, we could see the creature.
A mangy dog,
dear thing,
it's neck stretched almost to breaking
being dragged, dragged, dragged
across the concrete slabs of the station
next to the trains.

The trains steamy and snorting
the people rushing to and fro
the hawkers selling oranges peanuts
newspapers toys tea themselves.

Over it all
the howl of the dog
its eyes bulged out
blood bursting from the corners
of the eyes
its teeth bared
its tongue hanging out
its throat extended
dragged dragged dragged dragged
by a rope around its neck.

With all its weight resisting
to being pulled
Its back body a triangle
against the cement
Its legs with claws scraping

The man pulling this in pain beast
was indifferent.
Get this dog out of my station
was in his manner of pulling.
His soul was deaf to pain
of this dog.

He was doing what he was doing.

from "A Response to Maura Reilly's
'Taking the Measure of Sexism:
Facts, Figures, and Fixes'"

What an amazement that the lost, buried, denied, deflected history of women
artists has been irrevocably brought forward. This hard won integration of
feminist anthropology, archaeology, linguistics, religious studies and more,
established our suppressed inheritance, vivifying this great creative realm
formally identified as exclusively male. Even last month complex electronic
measurements confirmed that the patterns of handprints in paleolithic caves
were made by women (probably using menstrual blood). Women artists had
already recognized our marks from paleolithic, Cyclatic, up to and including
certain Eurocentric artworks and the reluctant recognition of noneuropean.

This richness was seized by feminist determinations in the 1970s when
women founded independent galleries, activist journals, public protests
against their exclusion. These achievements took unexpected power and
relevance. Nevertheless they remain fragile, precarious, subject to societal
upheavals. We who have the most functional aesthetic freedoms must extend
our capabilities to aid and abet women and women artists who's lives are
constrained, controlled, and often in danger.

In 1972 when I self-printed my feminist notes "Women in the Year 2000" I
could only hope that most of the creative intentions I described for our future
might become possible and have now come to fruition in our culture. I am
experiencing retroactive cautions given the degree of glamour, economic
reward, and current cultural embrace of many things feminist lacking rigor,
radicalization, and resistance. It brings to mind our feminist precedence,
radical artists who died in poverty and hunger such as Elsa Von Freytag-
Loringhoven. She might be considered the first body artist, an inspiration
for DaDa, Happenings and the current "selfie." The immensity of her
achievements were so shocking that they remain buried in some addendum
on eccentric art.

from *Jason and Shirley*

JASON [subject]: What did the Trenton county sheriff call the nigger that got shot fourteen times? The worst case of suicide he ever did see.

SHIRLEY [filmmaker]: Okay, cut. Think we have twenty good minutes. Okay? So we need ninety. Okay, so don't waste anymore time. . . .

SHIRLEY: Tell us about the time you were raped at Riker's Island.

JASON: You're asking me questions without any real meaning.

SHIRLEY: Why did you break your glasses and slit your wrists at Riker's?

JASON: Is this it? Is this the moment? This where Jason's supposed to break? This where Jason the puppet starts to dance and do whatever the director tells him to do? Is this what the director wants? Is this what we're here for?

SHIRLEY: Jason you wouldn't have broken your glasses if you thought you were gonna live.

JASON: It's the voice in my head that's driving me crazy. You're fuckin with me. I know you're fucking with my nerves and you're fucking with my endurance. Fucking with my consciousness.

SHIRLEY: Sorry, I - got -

JASON: And you're fucking with my peace of mind.

SHIRLEY: Tell them what the system did to you.

JASON: You're fucking, you're fucking me up!

SHIRLEY: You broke your glasses and slit your wrists!

JASON: You're fucking me up!

SHIRLEY: And you wanted to die!

JASON: You are fucking me up!

SHIRLEY: Because the system fucked you over!

JASON: What's the motherfucking system!? You want a system? What do you got you got your schedule, you got your fucking boom mic! Or whatever you fucking call them!

You got this—

SHIRLEY: You were trapped, you were humiliated,

JASON: Camera!

SHIRLEY: You were put into prison, you were raped—

JASON: And you're trying to get something out of me!

JASON: No, I was raped? You was raped!

SHIRLEY: Okay now we know, now we know the truth.

JASON: I'm a nigger. You're a nigger. He's a nigger. She's a nigger. We's a nigger. They's a nigger.

SHIRLEY: Now we know the truth and you know what the truth is? You won't tell the truth.

JASON: You wanna hear the truth? I'm a great big star but they will not admit it. And this is where the scene changes into a more classic Hollywood scene where she says, "You know how to whistle. You just pucker up your lips and blow."

JOHN (filmmaker): Roll out.

SHIRLEY: Okay everyone, take five.

Jason and Shirley (2015), directed by Stephen Winter

Runaway Shot

A number of citizens went on Wednesday evening to arrest fifteen to twenty
runaway slaves,
Slager follows him, reaching at the man with an object that appears to be a
Taser stun gun.
men and women who were encamped in the swamp in Fauberg Washington,
at the rear of the third municipality.
As Scott pulls away, the object falls to the ground, and Slager pulls out his
handgun as Scott runs away.
When they came on the camp, the negroes were preparing supper, and when
called on to surrender, ran off;
There is no indication that Scott was ordered to halt or surrender.
upon which those in pursuit fired, killed a man and a woman and wounded
two women;
The final shot sends Scott falling face-down about 30 feet away.
the others escaped.
Slager then slowly walks toward him and orders Scott to put his hands behind
his back, but the man doesn't move, so he pulls Scott's arms back and cuffs
his hands. The officer then walks briskly back to where he fired the shots,
speaking into his radio.

If White People
Didn't Invent Air

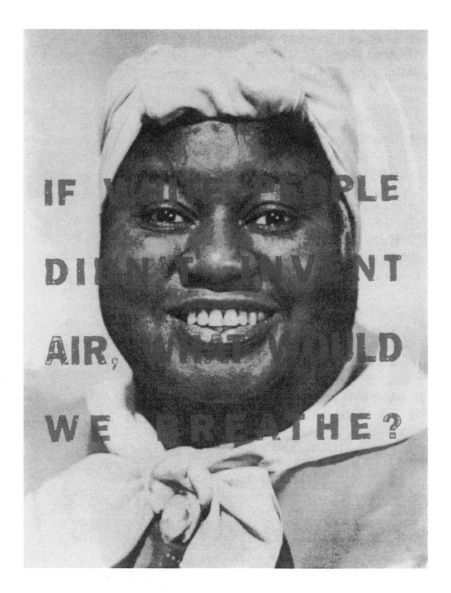

Poem

The primary catalysts for the decomposition of LSD are heat, light, oxygen, and moisture. LSD's shelf life can be significantly extended if exposure to these are minimized.

Air & Light

Keeping LSD in an air and light proof container is the most important step. A good option is a dark amber glass container kept somewhere cool. Remember, most plastic (plastic bags) is not air tight, though it's a lot better than nothing. Likewise, keeping blotter in foil isn't going to stop air transfer, but it's also better than nothing. If glass isn't available, a combination of foil and plastic would be more effective than either one alone.

Temperature

LSD will degrade even at room temperature, but the hotter the temperature and the longer it is stored in a hot location, the more it will degrade. At room temperature, degradation is quite slow, so a cool room, out of the sun is generally enough to minimize break-down. Storing blotter in the refrigerator or freezer is fine, but is probably unnecessary.

Moisture

If blotter is stored somewhere cold (as opposed to cool), it should be allowed to return to room temperature before being opened as this will prevent condensation from forming. Also, if the weather is extremely humid, storing LSD with a little bit of dessicant (drying agent), can ensure that it stays dry.

If these storage methods are followed, blotter should last for many years. Foil in the freezer is a common storage method, and should be effective at keeping degradation to a minimum for a few years.

JULIANA SPAHR

Went Looking and Found Coyotes

And there we were.

The light that fall was somewhat golden.

The trees held their leaves for longer than usual and it was warm in a cool sort of
      way.

There was a mist or a fog or a smoke that held us

And we walked with this mist or fog or smoke and amidst it also and we breathed
      it in, deep.

It cloaked us. From the inside.

That winter the wolf came.

Came to us. Came near to us. Walked toward this fog of us.

He was two and a half years old and he was the first one back.

He was alone. Wandering over mountains. Across highways. Through forests.

Back and forth he went. Alone.

He was looking for others.

They were not to be found.

Yet he was mutual, we noticed, he cavorted with coyotes.

What else could he do?

He was the only one, not as in the chosen one, but as one of the un-eradicated
      ones.

We called him OR7.

That winter, as OR7 walked to where we were, although not with any desire to be
      with us,

we waited for the mist, the fog, the smoke to turn into the rains,

saying to each other often that the rains are coming, surely the rains are coming.

But the rains never really came.

Or came so late that we barely noticed them.

When they arrived, we just put up a tarp and waited them out.

Together. There. Under the tarp. For a few minutes. Unevenly, there. But there.
      Together. Still.

That tarp is a version of what mattered. Together.

That winter, we were mainly men.

Not at first, but later,

At first, it was hard to say.

We were so many different things.

That was the idea.

By the end though, by winter, we were mainly men.

And those of us who were not men circled around each other unevenly.

Still learning though. Still. Together. We had no other choice.

That winter every time we wrote the word "interest" we replaced it with the word
"love."

That winter we just rhymed and rhymed on. Together. Using words. Together. That
winter everything suddenly written in our pentameters, our alexandrines,
our heroic couplets, which was often an associational sentence based
quiet line, one indebted to lyric in which the we stood in for the beloved
and yet there was almost never a description of this beloved, no listing
of their red lips, their firm breasts, their smooth skin, leaving a sort of
generic atmosphere.

I could tell you of the other things too.

A European influence.

A Middle Eastern influence.

A list of skirmishes.

A feeling of it being nothing. No wait, something. No see, nothing. Possibly
something. No. Nothing.

Let's just admit it.

We lost all the skirmishes, even the one called the PR war.

But that winter, we were there.

Under a tarp. Close. Together

Just dealing with. Together. Went looking and found coyotes.

[The last writing of me]

The last writing of me stopped somewhere around 2009. That's actually where I incorporated the 2.0 in (FHAK). It represents the second time of failure due to a lack of motivation alongside of disbelief. There've been so many changes in my life with a whirl world of pre-mature thinking as well as growth.

As I discovered little secrets about myself like different thoughts and how they never came to me in an organizational form, I subconsciously developed a thinking pattern from BACK–FRONT! I had a love for critical thinking without a clear understanding of what I was really doing. I never understood why my mother would never agree with me on such basic level of thinking opposed to what she felt was too much on me to grasp simply because of me being a visual learner and her not trusting my high school dropout years; she still had concerns of where my information was coming from.

I was a visionary by heart, in my own right, it was about being gifted. I stood on these ideas of being right in my own little ways. It was something that I decided to protect; I was sincere in not knowing, and still am. I never liked school as a kid.

I was a believer of what people said, word of mouth, which later I discovered was a job within itself. You had to defriciate logic from common sense with guys who made decisions similar to yours. Self-education wasn't popular in 1992–2000, nor was information accessible like you can find today. I was a magnet to intellectual quotes that came from guys who stood in the same pissy hallways as I did. We borrowed each other's ways that would later lead me into an institution of real knowledgeable brothers. These were considered to be the cool kids. Guys who would be put away over the next 20 years, that if ever given another opportunity, or shot at life, could rule a nation. Schools would have been built from a more sophisticated approach. I'm talking about the people they consider uneducated but with a memory of a tech developer. Self-educated, with the only availability of religion services and a law library. I'm telling you what brilliancy looks like on a human being who once lost hope; it's amazing! I walked around with mental crutches for a cool 15 years, which allowed me to grow intellectually, experientially, ideologically . . . whatever! I've seen a social-aesthetic pattern that has worked a number on me. I was caught in a ghetto of worlds that physically kept me confined; meanwhile, my mental left planet earth. This was the first step of me being misinformed or stupid for a lack of better words. To be sharing space with the "whatever or what'it'is" crowd wasn't supposed to make sense, at least not for this time period. What I was being taught falls under the law of ghetto nigga shit on a Harvard level, a legislation of anything goes and decision making that ruled with an iron fist. THEN the rush of my best friend shantez murder pulling the trigger on him, a white orange nj police officer. what tez was saying, he was riding for me. he wasn't going back to prison, wasn't no women there. outside of that, his son ya-ya was only 1 0r 3 years old. we not the problem FHAK! ORANGE POLICE DEPT is; the whole bullshit of who should be listening to whom. Trayvon Martin and Mike Brown would understand this conversation. I became numb to death. The justice department never shows up when they're supposed to, and I don't care anymore.

Nothing would really improve. In 2001 I was still decoding ways on how to become a decent human being. My brother Mario gave me non-verbal content on how to evaluate myself. Things started to take a turn. Ignorance became tedious. Education became a factor which I knew it would as time wasn't on our side. The drug game became a tuition check. I hadn't made my stop to prison yet to obtain my G.E.D., and the streets wasn't the place for that. I mean, how would I find time? The vows I made for the streets of Essex County as a young smart-ass wasn't nothing nice. I just got pulled from high school sometime ten years ago, and promised myself I would learn something every day. I still have to face my mother on the fact I need help with my decision making. She birthed me, but the streets fathered my understanding. A strong love-hate relationship that only benefited me when I had money in my pocket. I think I celebrated the day I was able to make an independent mental decision that eventually landed me in prison. I later found out my dad (the

streets) did a horrible job at parenting. How could my mother believe him—
he never was shit to begin with. She said, I act just like that creep. I wondered
if that's why she cared less. I still loved him. My son was three years old when
he first called me dad. My absence; not his . . .

I did nothing but read, educate myself, and later I would join the G.E.D.
program I never found time for on the streets. Whole time I'm thinking, what
can I do for my son to give him a better life? I just left a plantation that paid
me 6 cents a day for doing something I love, designing clothing (brown khaki
pants & shirts). So I'm not really excited about retail. My son needs me, and
I still haven't studied my weakness (drug sales), old friends who I still love,
and of course my father (the streets). He's going to support me to the day I
die, fck what my mother thinks. Then I thought about being a slave for 6 cents
a day and having my freedom and a chance to raise my son and be better than
I can imagine. I can live my childhood through him and teach him about
books and the prison yard education of the most influential inmates known
to man. My next thought was how can I make work fun? I have to put this
information to use. It's going to inspire somebody. I know it. I just don't know
who. Maybe my own people, but would they be interested? What if I spoke for
people who couldn't articulate words properly but enjoyed hearing me speak
up for them. Should I word it in a cool way so both parties can understand?
This would be something different that my ghetto (hood) will respect, or I
can teach it to hip hop culture, right? Artist respect artistry. I am an artist.
This is FHAK 2.0.

from "عملية Operación Opération Operation 行动 Операция"

Author's Note: This poem is composed of the names of military operations conducted by UN-member countries since the founding of the UN to the present day. The title is the word "operation" in each of the six official languages of the UN.

> *And now, O Muses, dwellers in the mansions of Olympus, tell me—*
> *for you are goddesses and are in all places so that you see all*
> *things, while we know nothing but by report*
> —Homer, *Iliad*, Book 2

> *The Purposes of the United Nations are:*
> *To develop friendly relations among nations based on*
> *respect for the principle of equal rights and self-determination*
> *of peoples, and to take other appropriate measures to*
> *strengthen universal peace*
> —United Nations, *Charter of the United Nations*
> (1945), Ch. I, Art. I (2)

1945

Medico
Mustard
Tableland
Blacklist
Blacklist 40
Masterdom
Freeborn
Clobber
Haystack

1946

Kipper/ Faggot
Olympic
Goodwood
Wallop
Asylum
Crossbow
Archery
Sandstone
Marriage
Blizzard
Hunger III
Bille
Wasp
Whisk
Trademark
Stork
Copyright
Tabarin
Marriages
Homing Pigeon
Honeybee

Epilogue
Ribbon
Freshman
Sam
Puff
Keynote
Nipoff
Swallow
Squeeze
Heartbreak
Outward
Castanets
Agatha
Crossroads
Keelhaul
Shark
Highjump
Mudlark
Woodpecker
Oasis
Retail
Pedestal
Octopus

1947

Astonia
Halberd
Blackcurrant
Old Lace
Mackerel
Abstract
Curfew
Inkpot
Tornado

Hunger 4
Folium
Sparkler
Sandfly
Westward Ho
Traffic
Stockpile
Dinner Party
Happy Return
Bad Sachsa/ Oberjoch
Cantonment
Roundabout
Polly
Crossline
Eastwind
Fleacomb
Wisła/ Vistula
Diagram
Eraze
Tiger
Product
Bluecoat
Totalize
Grand National
Léa
Windmill
Ceinture/ Belt
Varsity
Plunder
Veritable

1948

Greenford
Caravan

Smoke
Harness
Pinstripe
Double Quick
Plain Fare
Second Slip
Pickle
Journey's End
Snooker
Planet
Seahawk
Stress
Itzuv/ Stabilization
Hashmed / Destroy
נחשון/ Snakebird
Sandstorm
Harel
חמץ ביעור /Passover Cleaning
יבוסי/ Yevusi
חמץ / Leaven
יפתח / Open
Seanuts
מטאטא / Broom
Maccabi
Barak/ Lightning
Gideon
Kilshon /Pitchfork
Ben-Ami
שפיפון / Schfifon
Tinok/ Baby
Namel
Bin Nun Alef/ Nun's Son
פְּלֶשֶׁת/ Pleshet
Bin Nun Bet
Yoram
Balak

Firedog
Plainfire
Ferryboat
Kedem
דקל מבצע / Palm Tree
Anti-Farouk
דני מבצע / Danny
Brosh/ Cypress
מָוֶת מִבְצָע / Death to the Invader
שׁוֹטֵר / Policeman
גַּיְ "ס / G.I.'s
Little Vittles
גַּיְ "ס II / G.I.'s II
Double Cross
Bison/ Duck
Way to the Negev
Avak/ Dust
Polo
Pelican
Velvetta /Alabama
ההר. / Mountain
Yoav / Ten Plagues
Hiram
Easy
Shmone/ Eight
Lot
אָסָף / Assaf
Geranium
Velvetta II /Alabama II
Kraai/ Crow
Horev Ayin
הַתְחָלָה / Beginning

1949

Rusty
Magnet
Cowbane
Link
House Party
Subsmash
Artisan
Scrum Half
Exodus
Turnover
עובדה / Uvda
Union
Refine
Branmash

1950

Iceberg
Renault
Weary
Kidney
House Party II
Carat
Musgrave
Off Load
Pokpoong /Storm
Blue Heart
Epicure
Chién di.ch Biên giö / Border Zone

1951	1952
Accent	Purvey
Mikado	Robot
Basket	Aberdeer
Rockaway	Mainbrace
Osmund	Gondola
Chivalrous	Misty Day
Rodeo Flail	Thrush
French Pastry	Neutralise
Tannenberg	Joint
Ranger	Rotor
Killer	Eagle
Poster	Tigress
Ripper	Admaston
Courageous	Concubine
Tomahawk	Beechers Brook
Rugged	Dew
Greenhouse	Tumbler-Snapper
Bonn/ Wahnerheide	Blaze
Minden	Distemper
Commando	Nostril
Polecharge	
Buster-Jangle	
Tulipe/ Tulip	

the burden of being *bama*

it's living on
sawdust and shrimp paste
to save for diamonds

it's being a lustrous luna
in a bamboo tube
thinking 'how dainty i am!'

it's being a haystack fire
flaring suddenly
fading out swiftly

it's aching for the aunt
from the embrace of the mother

what's your key
majority in minor-c or minority in major-d
cease-fire in flat-b or cease-identity in sharp-g
give me a falsetto
let's improvise
no need for harmony

what would you choose
want, rage or ignorance
defeatism or maldevelopment
an increase in viral load or a decrease in internet speed
sexual preoccupation or self-denial
power cuts or power crazes
a bag of rice or an ounce of democracy
myopic blitheness, escapist wizardry and alchemy
syncretisation of incompatibilities
internalisation of irreconcilabilities

the four noble truths
the four oaths.........

....

....

the menu is endless
the die's been cast

your karma is you
life short
suffering tall
plenty of water
no fish, no fish at all

Of Worship and Flight

why did I read about a house of snakes
if I'm trying to ease my boy's newfound fear
of slithering gods — when confronted with what can't
be explained, the explanation invades its own mask —
explaining to itself — that it's okay to spend years
on what *can't* be explained, echo becoming mask

the unknown gathers attention *from* the known
when re-scrambling its mechanism *of* the known —
— say that again — into your filter
your proven escape oiled of temptation
by cover of sight — where wonder and risk meet,
is where I found the bluebird's wings

furiously attempting to divert the black snake
away from its nest, its home — a valley of
contradictions, here before me — a bird in place
of its color, a hidden nest far from danger
where fear is waiting — to rearrange
the brain's reception tangents, a schoolyard of saints

visitors — foreign or local, you choose — dressed in matching *neckerchiefs*,
listening to sonic deception, imported
from the Bronx, from id, from upstate New York
a fearful collection of *coming outters* — where to be
not-gender — is — asterisk — obsidian death star, in-the-closet beatheads,
frostyards, cageophiles, khlebnovians, anti-hallmark prognosticators, devil
stanza fanatics

the ear will pick the closest coil, to die
against the weakest throat — there was a hero
who believed that every curse he caught, was his
for everyone's failed blessings — the moment
he knew his gift would captivate a million lives,
is when he shifted fear to front and blue —

scared of what moves me away from what moves me —
say that again — echo retreats to worship
I am fear away from *out* to catch the *in* away from in —
the old poet reads of something of life from *this one*
of one other from *that one*, the *out* remains — as the category
of event — is its willingness to define *end* from *in*

Bang Bawl Bocconi Birds Unspaced

Idea Of The Revolving Woman — Born In Space + As, Of Form
Replaced Of Idealized Symetrics
+ Revolving Space, Ideas Of Transfor-oman, As Dynamism Wowan
As Woman — Intermorsed By Code + Idea, Revolves; Woman Appears
As Revolving Hand, As; Breast Over Hand 'Evolving Hip —
Of Woman — As Sculptured Form + Revolving
Idealized Tummy, Over Back
Revolu;

Swervical Phears, Enforced; Ideas,
Of Revolution Woman — As Formed, In Head + Spatial Isms
Down Back + (and) Fluid Ofs, Long Boned, Over Skin
Long Backed, Over Bone Idealized As Hand
Over Genital Idea, + Dynamism — Of Ideal Man, Born
In Movement — Space Of Ideal Anatomy, Imagined As Revolution;
Running, Hands Over Idealized Form — Boned Bone Discovers, Spatial
Dynamis;

WOWAM MAW SWAWAN NAWM WOWAM MAW SWAWAN NAWM

bone-anatom-ody imagines prone position
bent over knees by side hips on rear over prone legs
connect one over other in one some are in one are
some in some one are in none are others
in one some are in none are ones

Revolutions, Born In Space, — Ideas Are Revolutin'
As Motio'n, Born
In One;

SWAWAN NAWM WOWAM MAW
WOWAM MAW SWAWAN NAWM
SWAWAN NAWM WOWAM MAW
WOWAM MAW SWAWAN NAWM
SWAWAN NAWM WOWAM MAW
WOWAM MAW SWAWAN NAWM
SWAWAN NAWM WOWAM MAW
WOWAM MAW SWAWAN NAWM
SWAWAN NAWM WOWAM MAW
WOWAM MAW SWAWAN NAWM
SWAWAN NAWM WOWAM MAW
WOWAM MAW SWAWAN NAWM
SWAWAN NAWM WOWAM MAW
WOWAM MAW SWAWAN NAWM
SWAWAN NAWM WOWAM MAW
WOWAM MAW SWAWAN NAWM
SWAWAN NAWM WOWAM MAW
WOWAM MAW SWAWAN NAWM
SWAWAN NAWM WOWAM MAW
WOWAM MAW SWAWAN NAWM
SWAWAN NAWM WOWAM MAW
WOWAM MAW SWAWAN NAWM
SWAWAN NAWM WOWAM MAW
WOWAM MAW SWAWAN NAWM
SWAWAN NAWM WOWAM MAW
WOWAM MAW SWAWAN NAWM
SWAWAN NAWM WOWAM MAW
WOWAM MAW SWAWAN NAWM

Pain and Construction of Envy

Ink Blot

Third things we're
  digging now
  retain
  walk back
  Men are brownies
  flat world
Nothing else is
  made

Hand Across the Movement

recipe for strings
  the one time
That's a real, safe place
  girl's coat
  good things
You can't hurt me
  without having heard of an axis
Shut in front with army of
     lost birds
I don't know
     why
Something would break—

What Happened to the Myna Birds?

replenish
inspection
terms
might be seen
eventually
safety instructions
rib cage
Mike, the pond
can be seen.

Some Problem

Blond cover up – Come to the end – the invitation—
with approval – d'a full time – coming down –
a French palette – we're on the other side
Of the river – practical radical

Common Joys

pfst!, the yellow bag
Retink, Betsy
You have a new one,
   new vertical one
say, the word
One of the things I like
Eighth month
Give it a wind!
Much more than is necessary
Necklaces
You can cut it
walked in a hundred

Open Light
A little bit –
    just a mark
You wait here,
    for a dog
I like the color
    into the room
the same one who did
The whole thing in life.

In the Canary Yellow

Touch the path behind the trees
They didn't cook rice that way
Green service
He has the address

Walking Man

Fast – Food
Called, "friend"
glittering
some people's garden
-They all came in one
Are the kids calling you back?
                              -No.

What is a broken heart?
The clock
    Two million—
    types of poetry

Wild man-flew
   -courtesy
for a long time
I actually do

in the chamber, across the road

He looked you in the face
                with the same blood.

She Will Welcome You

in front of
regardless of the
NOT somebody
Looked at it
can be
odd position
Every twist and turn
Confrontation
in many, many ways,

no denial

no denial
no denial
no denial
no denial

no hunger, no hunger, no hunger
(oo oooo)

no denial, no hunger
no denial, no hunger
no denial, no hunger

no denial, no
no denial, no
no denial, no

Plot

The second stage is sleeplessness.
At first there was worry.
The third stage is "ordinary people."
The fourth: what to do.

The first stage is chaos.
The second is invention.
The steam engine. The napkin.
The picnic table. Money.

First you were walking across a bridge.
Then you were flying.
Then you were sweeping the floor.

First comes love.
Then nausea.

First pleasure.
Just a little pinch.

First the pupa, then the wings.
Wordlessness. Night.

The first thing is labor.
The second, we don't know.

First comes water.
Then air.
A hurricane. A sigh.
Abigail. Norma. Laquisha.
Molly. Sylvia. Roxanne.
Temperance. Emma. Delilah.
Daphne. Wilhelmina. Georgette.
Landfall. Rubble.

The first stage was childhood.
The second stage was Beatrice.

The first stage was Beatrice.
The second stage was hell.

First the city, then the forest.
The second stage was Virgil.
The third stage was expurgated.
The fourth went unnoticed.
The last stage was a letter.
A single meaningless hum.

What came first the money launderers or the flatterers.
What came first the Catherine wheel or the icebox.

In the beginning a voice.
In the beginning paramecia.

First carbon.
Then electricity.
Then shoes.

In the beginning a tree.

Before the house, a cave.
Before the cave, a swamp.
Before the swamp, a desert.

The garden was in the middle.
Between the sidewalk and the street.

In the beginning soup.

Then tables. The stock market.
Things on four legs.

In the beginning, I was frightened.
Then the darkness told a joke.

Which came first the river or the bank.
Which came first the priest or the undertaker.
Which came first crime or punishment.
Which came first the firemen or the cops.
Which came first conquest or discovery.
The fork or the spoon.
The point or the line-up.
The FBI or the CIA.

Which came first gravity or grace.
Which came first cotton or wool.
Which came first the slaver or the ship.
Which came first the ankle or the wing.
The hummingbird or the frog.
Puberty or ideology.

Which came first memory or forgiveness.
Which came first prohibition or women's suffrage.
Coffee or tea.

What came first yes or no.
What comes first silver or gold.
Porcelain or silk.
Pen or paper.

What came first Kyoto or Dresden.
What came first the renaissance or the reformation.
What would you rather be a rabbit or a duck.
Who is more powerful Mephistopheles or Marguerite.
Who's it going to be me or you.
What would you rather do burn or drown.

In the beginning I was invincible.
In the middle I came apart.

First there was a library then there was a café.
Then there was a wall of glass.

Which came first The Melancholy of Departure
Or the Double Dream of Spring.

Which came first repression or resistance.
Grammar or syntax.
The siren or the gunshot.
Which came first granite or marble.
The army or the drone.
The whistling or the blackbird.
Which came first sugar or rum. Pineapple or bananas.
The senate or the corporation.

Was the story half-empty or half-full.

What feels better pity or anger.

What scares you more life or death.

What describes you best, the steam in the engine or a penny on the tracks.

What were you thinking, a whimper or a bang.

What would you choose, a sandwich or a phonecall.

What did you expect, a question or an answer.

A piano or a clock.

Take all the time you want.

from *Some Worlds for Dr. Vogt*

XXXVIII

Make it new, then
erase it. Or, make it new
then do it again. To put your arm
through your arm, hand through
hand up to the shoulder
repeat with legs into
a letter, to make

a loudhailer of your head
to hover uneasily
as a geometry above
abstract planes, wings
as a swimmer uncrossed
against the air, as crosses
of propellers spin to suns.

XXXII

Not personal, this life
if you look out
over the tenements.
Original disappearing
act — a coming
that is not a going
for instance, in railway
tunnels, in
history, i.e., in what
happened before. Behind
the wheel, a rut, a
never finished thought.
Some thing to be
exact about, not easy
to say, or spit it out.
It's about to last
a long time
now, or
not at all.

Kaké!

Yeeeea Aaaaah
Yeeeea Aaaaah
Yeeeea Aaaaah
Yeeeea Aaaaah

Kaké!

Bump your occupation
Bump your education
We say we want world peace
But our dollar funds the rapin'

Even our durations
unify the nation
Recreate the government
or this world is 'bout to face it

[----]
disobey the system
keep that dollar in yo hand
and don't trust no politician

Recreate the Kongo
Don't buy no Monsanto
Watch out for Durango
'Cause he come with that commando, yah.

Yeeeea Aaaaah
Yeeeea Aaaaah
Yeeeea Aaaaah
Yeeeea Aaaaah

Kaké!

They call us the Third World
But the media are lying
How are we the Third World
When we sit on gold and diamonds?

Put us on the tv
Make us look so _____
Tell you take your dollar out
And then give it to the needy

How are we the needy
We got mangoes on the tree tree
I go to the big bush
If I want to take a pee pee

I still rep the Difa
Play it to the peepah
Stop your foreign aid
Africa's my self-help Africa, yah.

Yeeeea Aaaaah
Yeeeea Aaaaah
Yeeeea Aaaaah
Yeeeea Aaaaah

Kaké!

Africans have to watch the culture
We're surrounded by many vultures
Once you make your dollar go double
You just stepped in a world of trouble

Everybody wants to be cool
Africans weren't cool in my school
Maybe I can't entrust the rules

If you trust, then jump in this pool

Young P got the motive
Only Young P can't control it
I say Young P so you know it
Don't forget the name that's still growin'

'Cause once you give me your ears
There's shit you're not 'sposed to hear
This love I learned from my peers
Revolutionary right here, sakara.

Yeeeea Aaaaah
Yeeeea Aaaaah
Yeeeea Aaaaah
Yeeeea Aaaaah

Kaké!

BAX 2016 Acknowledgments

Samuel Ace: An audio version of "Private Prisons" previously appeared on *Textsound.org*.

Diana Adams: Oulipo-Pied Poems "#332," "#286," and "#321" first appeared in *Hello Ice* by Diana Adams, published by BlazeVOX Books.

Steven Alvarez: "tupontu" will appear in *The Codex Mojaodicus*, published by Fence Books and winner of the 2016 Fence Modern Poets Prize.

Mark Amerika: This excerpt from *Locus Solus* (2015) appears courtesy of Counterpath Press and the author.

Lesley Battler: "Peak Oil Exile" first appeared in *Endangered Hydrocarbons* (2015) by Lesley Battler. Reprinted with permission of BookThug and the author.

Christian Bok: "The Nocturne of Orpheus" first appeared in *The Xenotext* (*Book 1*), published in Toronto by Coach House Books (2015).

Anne Boyer: "The Animal Model of Inescapable Shock" previously appeared in *Garments Against Women* (Ahsahta, 2015). It was first published in *The New Republic*.

M. K. Brake: "Taxidermy for Dummies" first appeared in *TAGVVERK* on December 29, 2015.

Brandon Brown: "Zedd ft. Foxes, Clarity" first appeared in *Top 40* (Roof, 2014).

Lonely Christopher: These three poems are from *In a January Would*, an unpublished manuscript.

Maxwell Clark: "Prosodic Retardation" first appeared in +|+ (EPC Digital Editions, 2016)

Erik Didriksen: "[My mem'ry gazes back on young romance]" and "[I notice my beloved on thy arm]" first appeared in *Pop Sonnets: Shakespearean Spins on Your Favorite Songs,* published in October 2015 by Quirk Books (Philadelphia, PA) and HarperCollins UK (London, UK). Reprinted with permission of the author.

Craig Dworkin: This piece first appeared in *In Quire*, edited by H. L. Hix, on March 27, 2015.

Tim Fielder: Panels are taken from *Matty's Rocket Chapter 1: Ready for Blastoff!*, drawn and written by Tim Fielder and copyrighted by Dieselfunk Studios, 2015.

Tonya M. Foster: On July 20, 2015, "In Tongues" was published as a featured poem on The Academy of American Poets' Poem-A-Day site.

Peter Gizzi: "Song" is from *Archeophonics*, Wesleyan University Press (2016). It first appeared in *The Paris Review*.

Jody Gladding: "the spiders my arms," and "the hawthorn" originally appeared (as "Two Poems") in *ORION*.

Mira Gonzalez: Excerpt is taken from *Selected Tweets* (Short Flight/Long Drive Books, 2015).

E. Tracy Grinnell: "to list" is excerpted from "death / is an / innumerable / accuracy," published in *portrait of a lesser subject* by elis press (2015). The excerpt is reprinted by permission of the author.

Gabriel Gudding: "Amnicola" is excerpted from *Literature for Nonhumans* (Ahsahta, 2015). Portions of the poem were published previously in *Harper's Magazine, Action Yes*, and in the chapbook *Anthem for Temporal Measure* (Mansfield, 2010).

Joseph Harrington: "Cotton Still Tops in Area Economy" is excerpted from the e-chapbook *Goodnight Whoever's Listening* (Ithaca, NY: Essay Press 2015). I am grateful to the Millay Colony for the Arts for the time and space to compose the piece.

Jen Hofer: This excerpt is taken from *Intervenir / Intervene*, by Dolores Dorantes and Rodrigo Flores Sánchez, translated by Jen Hofer and published in Brooklyn, NY by Ugly Duckling Presse (2015).

Erica Hunt: "Should You Find Me" first appeared in *Time Sips Right Before the Eyes* (Belladonna, 2015). Copyrighted by the author.

Darius James and Tan Khanh Cao: "Light Headed" is excerpted from *Fever Water* by Tân Khánh Cao and Darius James, a limited edition artist's book, of which there are 150 numbered copies and which was published in 2015.

Patricia Spears Jones: "Self-Portrait as Shop Window" was first published *in A Lucent Fire: New & Selected Poems* (White Pine Press, 2015).

erika kaufman: "[how speech might help]" first appeared in the November 2015 issue of *The Brooklyn Rail*, edited by Anselm Berrigan.

Jake Kennedy: "Elegy for Harold Ramis" originally appeared in *Merz Structure No. 2 Burnt by Children at Play* (BookThug, 2015).

Sonnet L'Abbe: "XXIII" is forthcoming as part of "Three Ecolonizations from *Sonnet's Shakespeare*" in an upcoming issue of *ISLE: Interdisciplinary Studies in Literature and Environment*. "XXXIII" was first published in *The Revolving City: 51 Poems and the Stories Behind Them*, (Anvil Press, 2015). "LVII" was first published as part of a broadside called *From Sonnet's Shakespeare* by No Press in 2015.

George Lewis: "Soprano part for *Impromptu*" (completed 2012) was written for Ensemble Pamplemousse. It is previously unpublished and reproduced by permission of the composer.

Janice A. Lowe: "Boy Flower Tamir" is published in the collection *LEAVING CLE poems of nomadic dispersal* by Janice A. Lowe, Miami University Press (2016).

Corbin Louis: First I'd like to acknowledge my parents Mike and Linda Bugni for birthing me like an avalanche with a heart and then proceeding to save my life several times. That sounds like a lot of work. I'm grateful beyond words. But to use a few anyways, I love you. Thank you to my friends Andrew Pine, Amanda Hansen, Richard Barnard, Kyle Ricci, Tracy Gregory, Tim Luu, Amir Rassi, Erika Warren, so many more. It's been a hell of a ride.

Chris Mann: This work originally appeared on theuse.info.

Jimmy McInnes" "Begin Speech With" is an excerpt from *A More Perfect [*, published by BookThug in 2015. Earlier versions of this excerpt were published in the Summer 2012 issue of *The Puritan*, and in the chapbook *Begin Speech With*, published by FernoHouse in 2013.

Kevin McPherson Eckhoff: Parts of the selected work originally appeared in the following three publications: *their biography*, BookThug (2015); *LIT* 23, published by The New School (2013); *Dissections from their biography*, above/ground press (2012).

Wangechi Mutu: Video still is from *The End of Eating Everything*, an animated video released in 2013 (8 minute, 10 second loop) in an edition of 6. It was commissioned by the Nasher Museum of Art at Duke University, Durham, NC, and appears courtesy of the artist, Gladstone Gallery and Victoria Miro Gallery.

A.L. Nielsen: These poems first appeared in the journal *Hambone*, edited by Nathaniel Mackey.

Jenn Marie Nunes and Mel Coyle: Some of these poems have previously appeared in *Horseless Review* and/or in the chapbook *OPERA TRANS OPERA*, published by Alice Blue Books.

Barack Obama: Excerpt is taken from a speech commemorating the 50th anniversary of the Selma-Montgomery Marches, given on March 7, 2015 at the Edmund Pettus Bridge, Selma, Alabama. Reprinted from https://www.whitehouse.gov/the-press-office/2015/03/07/remarks-president-50th-anniversary-selma-montgomery-marches.

Julie Patton: The two pieces are taken from "Do Process" (1979 to present), a hand-altered, shorthair-head sculpture of a 630 page Gregg shorthand book from 1936.

Trace Peterson: "After Before and After" was previously published by *PBS Newshour, July 27, 2015, "Poet Creates First Class for Transgender Poetry"* and by *The Brooklyn Rail.*

Sina Queyras: "The Jailor" originally appeared in *The Walrus*

Aoife Roberts: "The Fact-Check" was included as a supplemental piece to *The Story of My Teeth* by Valeria Luiselli (Coffee House Press, 2015).

Lisa Robertson: "Notes on Form and Belief," the longer essay from which this text was excerpted, was published in July 2015 on the site *The Volta, in Evening will Come: A Monthly Journal of Poetics* (Affect Feature, edited by Julie Carr, issue 55). It was first given as a talk at Humber College, Toronto, for the Guelph Creative Writing MFA, at the invitation of director Catherine Bush.

Metta Sáma: "there is no flash" originally appeared on *poets.org*

James Sanders: "Plants (Jimmy Connors)" appeared in *Fence* (Winter 2016), and in *Self-Portrait in Plants* (Coconut Books, 2015). "Mesoscape" is forthcoming in *Symbiosis* (2016).

Jennifer Scappettone: This work was commissioned by Andrea Inglese for the collective exhibition *Descrizione del Mondo* at the Unione Culturale Antonicelli in Turin, Italy, which ran from March through August 2015. It subsequently appeared at the exhibition's virtual installation, based at http://www.descrizionedelmondo.it/. It will appear in *The Republic of Exit 43: Outtakes & Scores from an Archaeology and Pop-Up Opera of the Corporate*

Dump, forthcoming from Atelos Press. Grateful acknowledgment goes to the editors for their permission to republish.

Carolee Schneemann: The text was originally published in *Art News* (June 2015) as a response to Maura Reilly's "Taking the Measure of Sexism: Facts, Figures, and Fixes."

Sarah Schulman, Stephen Winter, Jack Waters: "Jason and Shirley" is from the 2015 feature film *Jason and Shirley,* directed by Stephen Winter, starring Jack Waters and Sarah Schulman. The script is by Stephen Winter, Jack Waters and Sarah Schulman. The film is a response to Shirley Clarke's 1966 experimental classic *Portrait of Jason,* the first representation of a black, gay man in cinema. *Jason and Shirley* had its world premiere at Brooklyn Academy of Music, and was reprised for a week run at the Museum of Modern Art. It has also been shown at Film Festivals in Los Angeles, San Francisco, and London, and at universities, community centers and museums, including the AGO in Toronto. For information about screenings, please contact Stephen Winter at stefelfilm@gmail.com.

Dread Scott: "Runaway Shot" uses text from *The Brooklyn Daily Eagle,* February 13, 1846 (originally printed in the *N.O. Jeffersonian*) and an article published on *CBSNews.com* on April 8, 2015.

Rod Smith: "Poem" by Rod Smith first appeared in *Touché* (Wave Books, 2015). The text, sans title, for "Poem" was taken from a website that has now disappeared, though the text can still be found on Bluelight, Erowid, Yahoo, and other webpages and message boards around the web.

Juliana Spahr: "Went Looking and Found Coyotes" originally appeared in *That Winter the Wolf Came* (Commune Editions, 2015).

Fakhair Spence: Thank you to my lovely girlfriend Tianah for always believing in me, staying up with me on them sleepless nights. Getting on her nerves about perfection and craftsmanship. To Shelagh for all the amazing ideas, bringing me to such great weird places mentally to see the bigger picture. Creating this world for me that I had no idea existed. Inspiring me to perfect my craft and implanting in my head enrolling at Harvard for the shits and giggles of it. To Dr. Stevens, who seen this vision in me long before I knew it was possible to bring it into a reality, allowing me to understand myself through perseverance. Holding up her office space like I paid rent. Educating me without ever taking a semester or having a degree to be so profound. My brother Mario, who's been my roll model since the age of seven, who told me about greatness and created stories for me that made me look at life from a penthouse point of view. To my neighborhood (my hood), I'm privileged to have a life of growing up on the 2nd floor, looking out my project window exploring my options on what I wanted to be in life. I only seen three choices, it was hoop dreams, be a hustler, or learn how to be influenced by my peers. Being able to survive and make it pass 18 years old was like four years of college, if you don't make it to the league, the chances are you'll return to the place that will kill you. My beautiful daughter who is a reflection of me (Kennedy Madison Spence), my twin, since she's been here on earth, nothing but blessings have been in my life. And last! My best friends who became strangers. I changed for greatness and they stay complacent now we just stop and stare like something that never once was. What a beautiful struggle. They say I changed, like I work this hard to stay the same. "[The last writing of me]" was originally published as part of a chapbook by belladonna*

ko ko thett: "the burden of being *bama*" first appeared in *World Literature Today* (University of Oklahoma) in January 2012. It was included in *Bones will Crow: Fifteen Contemporary Burmese Poets* [ARC (UK, 2012) & Northern Illinois University Press (NIUP, 2013)]. "the burden of being *bama*" is also a pocket-sized bilingual (English-Chinese), one of the twenty-two titles published for 2015 Hong Kong International Poetry Nights, by Chinese University Press Hong Kong.

Edwin Torres: "Of Flight and Worship" first appeared in Packingtown Review (Volume 7, 2015).

Elizabeth Willis: "Plot" first appeared in the *New Yorker*.

Matvei Yankelevich: "XXXIII" and "XXXVIII" first appeared in *Some Words for Dr. Vogt* (Black Square Editions, 2015).

About the Contributors

SAMUEL ACE is the author of three collections of poetry: *Normal Sex* (Firebrand Books, 1994), *Home in three days. Don't wash.* (Hard Press, 1996), and, most recently, *Stealth* (Chax Press, 2011), with poet Maureen Seaton. He is the recipient of a New York Foundation for the Arts Fellowship, a two-time Lambda Literary Awards finalist, a winner of the Astraea Lesbian Writers Fund Award and the Firecracker Alternative Book Award, and a finalist for the National Poetry Series. His work has been widely anthologized, and has appeared in or is forthcoming from *Plume, Aufgabe, Atlas Review, Mandorla, Versal, The Collagist, Troubling the Line: Genderqueer Poetry and Poetics,* and many other publications.

DIANA ADAMS is a writer from Edmonton, Alberta with work published in a variety of journals, including *Boston Review, Drunken Boat, Fogged Clarity, Oranges & Sardines, The Laurel Review,* and *Ekleksogaphia.* Her work has been included in several anthologies, including the *2009 Rhysling Anthology.* Her most recent books are *Hello Ice* (BlazeVOX, 2011), *Catch* (Corrupt Press, 2014), and *Lights on The Way Out* (Larry Fagin, 2016).

STEVEN ALVAREZ is the author of two novels-in-verse, *The Pocho Codex* (Editorial Paroxismo, 2011) and *The Xicano Genome* (Editorial Paroxismo, 2013). He has also authored two chapbooks, *Six Poems from the Codex Mojaodicus* (Seven Kitchens Press, 2014), winner of the Rane Arroyo Poetry Prize, and *Un/documented, Kentucky* (The Rusty Toque, 2016), winner of the 2015 Rusty Toque Chapbook Prize. His book *The Codex Mojaodicus* (Fence, 2016) won the Fence Modern Poets Prize. His work has appeared in *Best American Experimental Writing 2015, Berkeley Poetry Review, Drunken Boat, Fence, Huizache,* and *Waxwing.* He is an Assistant Professor of Writing, Rhetoric, and Digital Studies at the University of Kentucky.

MARK AMERIKA has exhibited his work at venues such as the Whitney Museum of American Art, the Denver Art Museum, the Institute of Contemporary Arts in London, and the Walker Art Center in Minneapolis. In 2009, he released *Immobilité*, generally considered the first feature-length art film ever shot on a mobile phone. He is the author of many books, including *The Kafka Chronicles* (FC2/University of Alabama Press, 1993), *Sexual Blood* (FC2/University of Alabama Press, 1995), *META/DATA: A Digital Poetics* (The MIT Press, 2007), *remixthebook* (University of Minnesota Press, 2011; remixthebook.com) and *Locus Solus* (Counterpath Press, 2014). Amerika is Professor of Art and Art History at University of Colorado Boulder, where he was recently appointed the Founding Director of the Doctoral Program in Intermedia Art, Writing, and Performance. More information can found at his website, markamerika.com, and at his Twitter feed (@markamerika).

JENNIFER BARTLETT is the author of three books of poetry and coeditor of the anthology *Beauty Is a Verb: The New Poetry of Disability* (Cinco Puntos Press, 2011).

LESLEY BATTLER has published her work in a wide range of literary journals, including *Arc, Contemporary Verse 2, dANDelion, filling Station, Prism International, West Coast Line,* and *Best Canadian Poetry 2015*. Her debut book of poetry is *Endangered Hydrocarbons* (BookThug, 2015). She currently lives in Calgary, Alberta, and no longer works in the petrochemical industry.

CHRISTIAN BÖK is the author of *Crystallography* (Coach House Books, 1994), a pataphysical encyclopedia nominated for the Gerald Lampert Memorial Award, and *Eunoia* (Coach House Books, 2001), a bestselling work of experimental literature, which won the Griffin Prize for Poetic Excellence. He is currently working on a project, *The Xenotext*, which involves the creation of "living poetry" through the encipherment of a text into the genome of a bacterium. Bök teaches English at the University of Calgary.

ANNE BOYER is the author of *Garments Against Women* (Ahsahta Press, 2015), *My Common Heart* (Spooky Girlfriend, 2011), and *The Romance of Happy Workers* (Coffee House Press, 2008). She lives in Kansas City.

M. K. BRAKE is the author of *The Taxidermist's Girl* (Dancing Girl Press, 2016). Her work can be found in *Fruita Pulp, Smoking Glue Gun, Bayou Magazine, TAGVVERK Journal,* and others. She holds an MFA in Poetry from Louisiana

State University and in fall of 2016 will begin an MFA in Nonfiction at the University of Iowa.

BRANDON BROWN is the author of several books, most recently *Top 40* (Roof Books, 2014) and *Flowering Mall* (Roof Books, 2012). In 2016, Big Lucks will publish *The Good Life,* a slim volume of poems. Brown is a coeditor at Krupskaya and occasionally publishes small press materials under the imprint OMG! His writing on art and culture in the Bay Area has appeared in *Open Space, Art Practical,* and *KQED Arts.* He lives in Oakland.

227

TÂN KHÁNH CAO is an artist named after a village in South Vietnam that may or may not still exist. She has worked at City Lights Bookstore in San Francisco for over a decade. Once a year, she collects green bowler hats and teeth.

LONELY CHRISTOPHER is a poet and filmmaker. He is the author of the poetry collection *Death & Disaster Series* (Monk Books, 2014) and the short story collection *The Mechanics of Homosexual Intercourse* (Akashic Books, 2011). His first novel, *THERE,* is forthcoming in 2017. His plays have been performed on both coasts and in Canada and China. His film credits include the feature *MOM* (which he wrote and directed), the shorts *We Are Not Here* and *Petit Lait* (which were adapted from his stories), and *Crazy House* (for which he wrote the screenplay). He lives in Brooklyn.

MAXWELL OWEN CLARK was born on October 29th, 1984. As early as 12, Clark began to suffer from crippling bouts of a major depression. He nonetheless somehow managed sometime after to attend college at the University of Vermont and then Yale, but in the midst of these studies suffered a very severe psychotic break. From then on he was not to go a year without hospitalization for intensely difficult psychiatric reasons and risk of suicide. His current diagnosis is "Psychosis (Not Otherwise Specified)." He has also spent the last decade of his life, since his psychotic break, as a painter, poet, and musician. He lives in New Haven.

MEL COYLE is from Chicago and other places where the corn grows. Her work appears in *ACTION YES, H_NGM_N, Alice Blue Review,* and *Leveler,* among others.

MARK Z. DANIELEWSKI was born in New York City and lives in Los Angeles. He is the author of the award-winning and bestselling novel *House of Leaves*, National Book Award finalist *Only Revolutions*, and the novella *The Fifty Year Sword*. The third installment of his 27-volume novel, *The Familiar*, was released in June 2016.

KEVIN DAVIES lives in Brooklyn. His books include *The Golden Age of Paraphernalia* (Edge Books, 2008) and *Comp* (Edge Books, 2000).

NATHANIEL DAVIS has had writing and translations published by The Last Books, Dalkey Archive Press, *Inventory*, *Cannon Magazine*, *SKULPI*, and WCW Gallery (Hamburg). He worked as editor for Dalkey Archive Press in Illinois and Texas, where he compiled the 2016 and 2017 editions of *Best European Fiction*. He lives in Paris and is finishing his first novel.

SAMUEL R. DELANY was born in 1942 in Harlem, then the black ghetto of New York City. He is a writer and critic who has published novels and essays and taught comparative literature, English, and creative writing at the University of Massachusetts Amherst, SUNY Buffalo, and Temple University. He began publishing science fiction in 1962 and has gone on to write comics, pornography, and graphic novels. He has written extensively on gay rights and lives with his daughter and son-in-law outside of Philadelphia, along with his partner of twenty-seven years, Dennis Rickett. His books include works of fiction, such as *Nova* (Doubleday, 1968), *Dhalgren* (Bantam, 1975), *Tales of Nevèrÿon* (Bantam, 1979), and *Dark Reflections* (Carroll & Graf, 2007); nonfiction books, such as *Time Square Red, Times Square Blue* (New York University Press, 1999); a creative writing textbook, *About Writing* (Wesleyan, 2006); an autobiography, *The Motion of Light in Water* (University of Minnesota Press, 2004); as well as the long science fiction novel, *Through the Valley of the Nest of Spiders* (Magnus Books, 2012). After many years in New York City, he has recently retired to live outside of Philadelphia. The first volume of his selected journals, *In Search of Silence, 1957-1968*, was edited by Kenneth R. James and will be published by Wesleyan in 2016.

ERIK DIDRIKSEN is a software engineer, musician, sonneteer, and trivia enthusiast. His book *Pop Sonnets: Shakespearean Spins on Your Favorite Songs* was published in 2015 by Quirk Books, and was a finalist for a Goodreads Choice Award. He lives in Astoria, New York.

CRAIG DWORKIN is the author of several books, most recently the poetry collections *Chapter XXIV* (Red Butte Press, 2013), *An Attempt at Exhausting a Place in Williamstown* (Publication Studio, 2015), and *Alkali* (Counterpath, 2015). He has also published two scholarly monographs, *Reading the Illegible* (Northwestern University Press, 2003) and *No Medium* (MIT Press, 2013). Recent coedited collections include *The Sound of Poetry/The Poetry of Sound* (The University of Chicago Press, 2009), *Against Expression: An Anthology of Conceptual Writing* (Northwestern, 2011), and *Nothing: A User's Manual* (Information as Material, 2015). He teaches literature and theory at the University of Utah and serves as Founding Senior Editor to Eclipse (eclipsearchive. org).

TIM FIELDER is a New York City-based illustrator, concept designer, cartoonist, animator, and instructor, as well as the creator of *Matty's Rocket* (Dieselfunk Studios, 2015).

RICHARD FOREMAN has directed, written, and designed seventy stage productions in America and abroad since 1968. He has received many awards, and has published nine books. He now works exclusively in experimental film.

TONYA M. FOSTER is the author of *A Swarm of Bees in High Court* (Belladonna*, 2015) and coeditor of *Third Mind: Creative Writing through Visual Art* (Teachers & Writers Collaborative, 2002). A poet and scholar, her writing and research focus on ideas of place and emplacement, and on intersections between the visual and the written. A recipient of awards from the Mellon Foundation, Ford Foundation, New York Foundation for the Arts, and the Macdowell Colony, her poetry, prose, and essays have appeared in *Callaloo, Tripwire, boundary2, MiPOESIAS*, and elsewhere. She is an Assistant Professor of Writing & Literature at California College of the Arts.

PETER GIZZI is the author of six collections, including *Threshold Songs* (Wesleyan, 2011) and *The Outernationale* (Wesleyan, 2008), as well as numerous chapbooks and artist-books. In 2014 Wesleyan published a retrospective volume, *In Defense of Nothing: Selected Poems 1987-2011*. His honors include the Lavan Younger Poet Award from the Academy of American Poets and artist grants from the Foundation for Contemporary Arts, The Howard Foundation, and the Guggenheim Foundation. He is currently the Judith E. Wilson Visiting Fellow in Poetry at Cambridge University. See petergizzi.org for more information.

JODY GLADDING's work explores the places where language and landscape converge. Her most recent poetry collection is *Translations from Bark Beetle* (Milkweed Editions, 2014). She has also translated thirty books from French. The poems appearing here are part of a new collection forthcoming from Ahsahta Press.

MIRA GONZALEZ was born in 1992 and lives in Venice, California. Her first book, *I Will Never Be Beautiful Enough to Make Us Beautiful Together* (Sorry House, 2013) was shortlisted for the Believer Poetry Award. She was also nominated for another award, but lost to the guy who wrote *Lord of the Rings*.

JEAN GRAE is a polymath. She is a critically acclaimed lyricist, producer, writer, comedian, director, cinematographer and all around consummate entertainer who has been challenging the boundaries of artistry since her debut in 1996. Establishing herself first as an iconic figure in hip-hop and amassing an international fan base, she has worked alongside Mos Def, Talib Kweli, The Roots, Robert Glasper and 80 million other people you like. In just the past 2 years, she has independently released 9 albums, a book, an audiobook, and created her own webseries, "Life With Jeannie." Grae also has her semi-regular cooking column for *Jezebel* and has been a guest writer for such publications as *BUST* and CNN's *Eatocracy*. We'd tell you more, but there isn't time. Jean really needs to relax.

E. TRACY GRINNELL is the author of *Hell Figures* (Nightboat Books, 2016), *portrait of a lesser subject* (elis press, 2015), *Some Clear Souvenir* (O Books, 2006), and *Music or Forgetting* (O Books, 2001). *Helen: A Fugue* was published in the first volume of the Belladonna Elders Series (2008) in conversation with *A Pear / Actions are Erased* by Leslie Scalapino. Grinnell's poetry has been translated into French, Serbian, and Portuguese. She currently teaches in the MFA Writing Program at Pratt Institute and lives in Brooklyn, New York. She is the founding editor and director of Litmus Press.

GABRIEL GUDDING is the author of *Literature for Nonhumans* (Ahsahta Press, 2015), *Rhode Island Notebook* (Dalkey Archive Press, 2007), and *A Defense of Poetry* (University of Pittsburgh Press, 2002). His essays and poems appear in such periodicals as *Harper's Magazine, The Nation,* and *Journal of the History of Ideas,* and in such anthologies as *Great American Prose Poems, Best American Poetry,* and *&Now: Best Innovative Writing.* His translations from Spanish appear in anthologies such as *The Oxford Book of Latin American Poetry, Poems for the Millennium,* and *The Whole Island: Six Decades of Cuban Poetry.* His essays and poems have been translated into French, Spanish, Portuguese, Danish, and Vietnamese. He teaches in the Creative Writing and Literature & Cultural Studies programs at Illinois State University.

JOSEPH HARRINGTON is the author of *Things Come On (an amneoir)* (Wesleyan, 2011), a *Rumpus* Poetry Book Club selection; the chapbooks *Goodnight Whoever's Listening* (Essay Press, 2015) and *Earth Day Suite* (Beard of Bees, 2010); and the critical work *Poetry and the Public* (Wesleyan, 2002). His creative work has appeared in *Bombay Gin, Eleven Eleven, Colorado Review, 1913: a journal of forms, Fact-Simile,* and elsewhere. He teaches at the University of Kansas in Lawrence.

JEN HOFER is a Los Angeles-based poet, translator, social justice interpreter, teacher, knitter, book-maker, public letter-writer, urban cyclist, and co-founder of the language justice and language experimentation collaborative Antena and the local language justice advocacy collective Antena Los Ángeles. She publishes poems, translations, and visual-textual works with numerous small presses, including Action Books, Atelos, belladonna, Counterpath Press, Kenning Editions, Insert Press, Les Figues Press, Litmus Press, LRL Textile Editions, NewLights Press, Palm Press, Subpress, Ugly Duckling Presse, Writ Large Press, and in various DIY/DIT incarnations. Her most recent translations are *Intervenir/Intervene,* by Dolores Dorantes and Rodrigo Flores Sánchez (Ugly Duckling Presse, 2015) and *Estilo/Style* by Dolores Dorantes (Kenning Editions, 2016).

ERICA HUNT is a poet and essayist. Her latest work is published in *The Literary Review, boundary 2*, and the anthology *What I Say: Innovative Poetry by Black Writers in America* (University of Alabama Press, 2015), edited by Laurie Ramey and Aldon Nielson. In 2015, Hunt gave the inaugural Leslie Scalopino lecture at Pratt Institute's MFA Program in Poetics, titled "On Pronouns: I, You, We, with an aside on Zi and They."

DARIUS JAMES is isolated in a southeastern corner of Connecticut. He is there until his head explodes in a Technicolor shatter of bone and blood from lack of electrical stimulation to the synapses in his brain's cerebral cortex. Over the years, he has written for a number of publications, including *The Village Voice, Vibe, The New York Times Magazine, Details*, and *Puritan*. He is most proud of appearing on the cover of Al Goldstein's *Screw* for absolutely no discernible reason at all. Disgusted with Manhattan by the nineties, he moved to Berlin, Germany, and lived there for ten years. He had a pretty good time. He published books, including *Froggie Chocolates' Christmas Eve* (Verbrecher Verlag, 2003). He did internet radio ("Dr. Snakeskin's Voodoo Kitchen") with a gang of German hackers led by a Chicana from New Mexico. He appeared on German television. He wrote and directed theater performances (*Shadow of the SpiderWoman*). He also wrote, narrated, and guided the documentary *The United States of Hoodoo*. Unfortunately, his father died in 2007 and cut his stay short. Now, he is composing a shamanistic text for a spoken word album. You also might have read his first novel, *Negrophobia* (St. Martin's Griffin, 1993).

PATRICIA SPEARS JONES is a Brooklyn-based African American poet and author of *A Lucent Fire: New and Selected Poems* (White Pine Press, 2015) and seven other poetry collections and chapbooks. Her works are anthologized widely, including in *Best American Poetry* and *Black Nature: Four Centuries of African American Nature Poetry* (University of Georgia Press, 2009). She is contributing editor to *BOMB* magazine, and in 2009 edited its anthology *THINK: Poems for Aretha Franklin's Inauguration Day Hat*. She is a senior fellow at Black Earth Institute, where she edited a recent issue of *About Place Journal*. She is recipient of a Barbara Deming Fund award as well as awards from the Goethe Institute, the Foundation for Contemporary Art, and the New York Community Trust; she has received grants from both the NEA and the New York Foundation for the Arts. She teaches for CUNY.

ERICA KAUFMAN is the author of *INSTANT CLASSIC* (Roof Books, 2013) and *censory impulse* (Factory School, 2009). she is also the coeditor of *NO GENDER: Reflections on the Life and Work of kari edwards* (Venn Diagram, 2009) and *Adrienne Rich: Teaching at CUNY, 1968–1974* (Lost & Found: The CUNY Poetics Document Initiative, 2014). she is the Director of Faculty and Curriculum Development for Bard College's Institute for Writing & Thinking and teaches in both its Master of Arts in Teaching and First Year Seminar Programs.

JAKE KENNEDY has studied at the Famous Philosophers' School and currently works at Okanagan College, Kelowna, BC, Canada.

MYUNG MI KIM is the author of a number of books, including *Penury* (Omnidawn Publishing, 2009), *DURA* (Nightboat Books, 2008), *Commons* (University of California Press, 2002), and *Under Flag* (Kelsey Street Press, 2008), winner of the Multicultural Publisher's Exchange Award. She has received fellowships and honors from the Djerassi Resident Artists Program, Gertrude Stein Awards for Innovative North American Poetry, and the Fund for Poetry. Kim is Professor of English and Director of the Poetics Program at the University at Buffalo, State University of New York.

MICHAEL KIRBY is a writer based in New York.

SONNET L'ABBÉ is a poet, essayist, and public speaker. The author of two collections of poetry, *A Strange Relief* (McClelland & Stewart, 2001) and *Killarnoe* (McClelland & Stewart, 2007), L'Abbé was the editor of *Best Canadian Poetry 2014* and was the 2015 Edna Staebler Writer in Residence at Wilfrid Laurier University. She has taught creative writing at the University of British Columbia-Okanagan and at the University of Toronto's School of Continuing Studies. L'Abbé currently teaches creative writing and English at Vancouver Island University. The poems included in this anthology are three erasures-by-crowding from her current project, *Sonnet's Shakespeare,* in which she overwrites or "colonizes" all 154 of Shakespeare's sonnets.

MONROE LAWRENCE was born in British Columbia, Canada. He lives in Providence, Rhode Island, where he studies in the MFA program at Brown University.

GEORGE E. LEWIS is the Edwin H. Case Professor of American Music at Columbia University. A fellow of the American Academy of Arts and Sciences, Lewis's other honors include a MacArthur Fellowship (2002) and a Guggenheim Fellowship (2015). A member of the Association for the Advancement of Creative Musicians (AACM) since 1971, Lewis's creative work has been presented by the BBC Scottish Symphony Orchestra, London Philharmonia Orchestra, Radio-Sinfonieorchester Stuttgart, International Contemporary Ensemble, and others. His book *A Power Stronger Than Itself: The AACM and American Experimental Music* (University of Chicago Press, 2008) received the American Book Award.

TAN LIN is the author of over twelve books, most recently, *Heath Course Pak, Insomnia and the Aunt*, and *7 Controlled Vocabularies and Obituary 2004. The Joy of Cooking*. His non-fiction writing has appeared in *the New York Times Book Review, Art in America, Artforum, Purple, Cabinet, and Triple Canopy*. He is the recipient of a 2012 Foundation for Contemporary Arts Grant, a Getty Distinguished Scholar Grant, and a Warhol Foundation/Creative Capital Arts Writing Grant. His art and video works have been screened at numerous museums, including MoMA/PS 1, Yale Art Museum, New Museum, and the Drawing Center. *7 Controlled Vocabularies* received the Association for Asian American Studies Award for Poetry/Literature. He is currently working on a novel, *Our Feelings Were Made By Hand*.

JANICE A. LOWE is a poet, composer and performer. She is the author of *LEAVING CLE, poems of nomadic dispersal* and the chapbook *SWAM*. Her poems have appeared in *Callaloo, American Poetry Review, The Hat, In the Tradition, The Poetry Project Online* and is featured on a digital album with Drew Gardner's Poetics Orchestra. She composed the musicals *Lil Budda,(Text by Stephanie L. Jones), Sit-In at the Five & Dime, (Words by Marjorie Duffield)* and *Somewhere in Texas, (Book and Lyrics by Charles E. Drew, Jr.)*. She has composed for the plays 12th and Clairmont by Jenni Lamb, The Super Starlet Shero Show by The Jones Twins and Door of No Return by Nehassaiu deGannes. She is a co-founder of The Dark Room Collective and has performed with the experimental bands w/o a net, HAGL and Digital Diaspora.

CORBIN LOUIS is a poet and performer from Seattle, Washington. At age 13 Corbin found his voice in rap and spoken word. By 2008 Corbin Louis became the Seattle Youth Poetry Slam Champion in a citywide competition. He is a recording artist and MFA student at University of Washington Bothell. Corbin's work has previously been featured in *Clamor Magazine, Atticus Review* and The Visible Verse Film Festival. The author seeks to extend stage performance through design mediums and visual rhythm. Ink becomes saliva and sweat. Salt water and whispers. The poet lives!

CHRIS MANN: language is the mechanism whereby you understand what i'm thinking better than i do (where i is defined by those changes for which i is required).

D. S. MARRIOTT is a poet and critic and is the author of *Haunted Life* (Rutgers UP, 2007), *On Black Men* (Columbia UP, 2000), and his most recent collections of poetry include: *In Neuter* (Equipage, 2013) and *The Bloods* (Shearsman Books, 2011). He currently teaches at the University of California, Santa Cruz.

JIMMY MCINNES was born and raised on Ontario's Bruce Peninsula. His first book of poetry, *A More Perfect [*, was released by BookThug in 2015. His poetry has appeared in *This Magazine, The Puritan, Descant,* the *Capilano Review Web Folio*, and *Poetry Is Dead*. His work has been shortlisted for the Great Canadian Literary Hunt and the Robert Kroetsch Award for Innovative Poetry. He currently lives in Toronto.

KEVIN MCPHERSON ECKHOFF sometimes oogy-boogies and othertimes ugga-wuggas. He has been shortlisted for the Relit Award and the Robert Kroetsch Award for Innovative Poetry. Jake Kennedy is his bestfriend for life, and together they collaborate on all sorts of literary shenaniganery, from unpoem performances to guest editing deathbed issues of Canadian periodicals. kevin lives in British Columbia with a mommoo, two boys, three dogs, and a hedgehog.

K. SILEM MOHAMMAD is the author of several books of poetry, including *Deer Head Nation* (Tougher Disguises, 2003), *Breathalyzer* (Edge Books, 2008), and

The Front (Roof Books, 2009). He teaches creative writing at Southern Oregon University, where he also edits *West Wind Review.*

WANGECHI MUTU was born and raised in Kenya and has made Art in New York for almost twenty years. Her work in multi-mediums has peeled into the deep layers that define gender and racial identity. At the center of her work she often places a performing or posed figure and uses this as a means of focal point and to unlock the dialogue about perception in both personal and political realms. She's primarily interested in how identity pivots around a kind social contract that can only be broken through personal and political re-invention and a re-writing of the codes that have been used to represent us. Her work proposes the need for a multiple-consciousness and an awareness of identity as performance, to be able to re-make the rules that bind our imagination. In order to reorganize the reality that serves us unsavory images of ourselves Mutu creatively dismantles old tropes and intricately pieces together new ones. Through performance, collage paintings, video and sculpture she continues to think about the complicatedness of being and how essentially one's physical body plays such a huge role in determining their experiences, their survival and ability to understand what that is. Wangechi Mutu is the recipient of the United States Artist Grant (2014), the Brooklyn Museum's Asher B. Durand Artist of the Year Award (2013), and was honored as Deutsche Bank's first Artist of the Year (2010). She has had solo exhibitions at the Museum of Contemporary Art Australia; Deutsche Guggenheim, Berlin; the Brooklyn Museum of Art; Montreal Museum of Contemporary Art; San Francisco Museum of Modern Art; Staatlichen Kunsthalle Baden-Baden, Germany; Wiels Contemporary Art Center, Brussels; the Nasher Museum of Art at Duke University, North Carolina; the Block Museum of Art at Northwestern University, Illinois; and Miami Art Museum. Mutu recently participated in the Venice Biennale: All the World's Futures (2015), the Dak'Art Biennial, the Kochi-Muziris Biennial, the Paris Triennial: Intense Proximity, the International Center of Photography's Triennial and the Moscow Biennale. Her work is included in the collections of the Museum of Modern Art, New York; The Whitney Museum of American Art; The Studio Museum in Harlem; The Museum of Contemporary Art, Chicago; the Museum of Contemporary Art, Los Angeles; the Nasher Museum of Art at

Duke University; the Montreal Museum of Contemporary Art; the Brooklyn Museum; and Tate Modern in London.

A. L. NIELSEN was the first winner of the Larry Neal Award for poetry, and is also the recipient of the Darwin Turner Award, the Josephine Miles Award, the SAMLA Studies Prize and the Kayden Award. His collections of poetry include *Heat Strings, Evacuation Routes, Stepping Razor, VEXT, Mixage, Mantic Semantic* and *A Brand New Beggar. Tray*, from which these selections were drawn, is forthcoming from Make Now Press. Nielsen serves as the George and Barbara Kelly Professor of American Literature at Penn State University. His volumes of criticism include *Reading Race, Writing between the Lines, C.L.R. James: A Critical Introduction, Black Chant* and *Integral Music: Languages of African American Innovation*. With Lauri Ramey he has edited two anthologies of experimental poetry by African American Poets, *Every Goodbye Ain't Gone* and *What I Say*.

JENN MARIE NUNES is the author of numerous chapbooks, including the forthcoming collection of short shorts, *JUNED*, winner of the YesYes Books 2015 Vinyl 45s Chapbook Contest. Her work appears in such journals as *ACTION YES, Black Warrior Review, Ninth Letter, DREGINALD* and *PANK*. Her first full-length collection, *AND/OR*, was the winner of the Switchback Books' Queer Voices Award.

BARACK OBAMA is the 44th President of the United States of America.

Born and raised in Brooklyn, SHELAGH PATTERSON is a poet, scholar, and activist. A recipient of the Bronx Writers' Center's Literary Arts Fellowship, a Cave Canem fellow, and a Scholar/Artist in Residence at the Urban Issues Institute at Essex County College, her poems have appeared in anthologies, newspapers, magazines, journals, experimental theatre, bureaucratic documents, and a feature film. Currently an Assistant Professor of English at Montclair State University, Shelagh lives in Newark, NJ.

JULIE EZELLE PATTON's chance based performances and ephemeral installations mine the hear, say and see shores between image, text, sound, and movement. Patton's most recent bound-ink-to-paper production is *Notes for Some (Nominally) Awake* (Yo Yo Labs). In 2015, Julie was honored with a Foundation for Contemporary Arts Grants to Artists award and an Atlantic Center for the Arts Master Artist Residency.

TRACE PETERSON is a trans woman poet critic. Author of *Since I Moved In* (Chax Press) and numerous chapbooks of poetry, she is Editor/Publisher of *EOAGH* and co-editor of the anthology *Troubling the Line: Trans and Genderqueer Poetry and Poetics* (Nightboat), which was a 2014 Lambda Literary Award Finalist. Her recent writing appears in *TSQ: Transgender Studies Quarterly, The Brooklyn Rail, The Ashbery Home School Gallery*, and the "Genre Queer" issue of *Cream City Review*. She currently serves on the Board of Directors for VIDA: Women in Literary Arts and teaches the first-ever course in Transgender Poetry at Hunter College.

SINA QUEYRAS lives in Montreal. *My Ariel* is forthcoming from Coach House Books in 2017.

AOIFE ROBERTS earned her MA in Literary Translation from City University London, and her BA in French & Performing Arts from the University of Sussex. She has been involved with organizations including Milkweed Editions, Coffee House Press, Rain Taxi, and 2dcloud, and has lived in Minneapolis, Luxembourg, Brighton, Quebec, London, and Brussels.

LISA ROBERTSON, a Canadian poet, essayist and translator, began publishing in the early '90s in Vancouver. Her books include *Debbie: An Epic, The Weather, The Men, R's Boat, Lisa Robertson's Magenta Soul Whip*, and *Cinema of the Present. Three Summers* is forthcoming. She has two collections of essays, *Nilling*, and *Occasional Works and Seven Walks from the Office for Soft Architecture*. With Matthew Stadler she co-edited and annotated *Revolution: A Reader*, a 1200-page proposition about being and resistance. She has worked as a visiting writer and teacher in Canada, the US, France, the Netherlands, and the UK. She lives in France.

METTA SÁMA is author of *the year we turned dragon, le animal and other creatures, After After/After "Sleeping to Dream," Nocturne Trio* and *South of Here.*

Her poems, fiction, creative non-fiction, literary scholarship & book reviews have been published in various literary journals and anthologies. Sáma is a Black Earth Institute fellow and a member of the Cave Canem Board; she is on the Advisory Board of Black Radish Books. Sáma received her MFA and MA from Western Michigan and her PhD from SUNY-Binghamton; she is Director of Center for Women Writers, Assistant Professor & Director of Creative Writing at Salem College.

JAMES SANDERS is a member of the Atlanta Poets Group, a (slowly atrophying) writing and performing collective. His most recent book is *Self-Portrait in Plants* from Coconut Books. The University of New Orleans Press also recently published the group's collection, *An Atlanta Poets Group Anthology: The Lattice Inside*.

JENNIFER SCAPPETTONE's work with languages spans scholarly and creative modes of inquiry, and a variety of media. Poetry collections include *From Dame Quickly* (Litmus, 2009) and *The Republic of Exit 43: Outtakes & Scores from an Archaeology and Pop-Up Opera of the Corporate Dump*, forthcoming from Atelos Press. She edited and translated *Locomotrix: Selected Poetry and Prose of Amelia Rosselli* (University of Chicago Press, 2012). Her most recent book is *Killing the Moonlight: Modernism in Venice* (Columbia University Press, 2014). She is currently sharing a Mellon Fellowship with Caroline Bergvall and Judd Morrissey at the Gray Center for Arts and Inquiry to work on a project called *The Data That We Breathe*.

RICHARD SCHECHNER is a professor of Performance Studies at NYU. He is editor of *TDR*. His books include *Environmental Theater, The End of Humanism, Between Theater and Anthropology, Performance Theory, Performance Studies An Introduction*, and *Performed Imaginaries*. His theatre productions have been seen in the USA, Romania, Poland, France, India, China, Taiwan, the UK, and the Republic of South Africa. He writes poetry and short fiction.

CAROLEE SCHNEEMANN, a multidisciplinary American artist, transformed the definition of art, especially discourses on the body, sexuality, and gender. The history of her work is characterized by research into archaic visual traditions, pleasure wrested from suppressive taboos, the body of the artist in dynamic relationship to the social body. Schneemann's work has been collected and shown at innumerable venues around the world. Her recent retrospective at the Museum der Moderne in Salzburg, Austria, curated by Sabine Breitwieser, includes over 350 works and is accompanied by a catalogue raisonee titled *Kinetic Painting. Carolee Schneemann: Unforgiveable* was released by Black Dog Publishing in November 2015. Schneemann's work was the focus of the fifth season of The Artist's Institute, New York. In 2015 MoMA, New York, acquired her canonical painting construction *Four Fur Cutting Boards,* as well

as *EyeBody: 36 Transformative Actions for Camera.* In 2016, Schneemann's work will be included in *From the Collection: The 1960s* at MoMA, New York, and *Postwar – Art between the Pacific and Atlantic 1945 – 1965*, Haus der Kunst, Munich, Curated by Okqui Enwezor. *Breaking the Frame*, a portrait of the artist's life and work by Marielle Nitoslawska, had its premiere at the New York Film Festival. Her work is represented by PPOW Gallery, and Gallery Lelong, which will mount two concurrent exhibitions of her work in the fall of 2016. Schneemann is the recipient of many grants and awards, including a Guggenheim Fellowship, a Gottlieb Foundation Grant, a National Endowment for the Arts Fellowship, a Rockefeller Foundation Fellowship, a Lifetime Achievement Award from the College Art Association, and the 2014 Aurora Award.

SARAH SCHULMAN's most recent books are the novel, *The Cosmopolitans* (Feminist Press) and the nonfiction book *Conflict Is Not Abuse: Overstating Harm, Community Responsibility, and the Duty of Repair* (Arsenal).

DREAD SCOTT is an interdisciplinary artist whose work is exhibited internationally. For three decades he has made work that encourages viewers to re-examine cohering norms of American society. In 1989, the US Senate outlawed one of his artworks and President Bush declared it "disgraceful" because of its use of the American flag. His art has been exhibited/performed at MoMA/PS1, Pori Art Museum (Finland), Brooklyn Academy of Music and galleries and street corners across the country. He is a recipient of grants from Creative Capital Foundation and the Pollock Krasner Foundation. His work is in the collection of the Whitney Museum.

ROD SMITH is the author of *Touché* (Wave Books, 2015), *What's the Deal?* (Song Cave, 2010), *Deed* (University of Iowa Press, 2007), and several other books. He edits the journal *Aerial*, publishes Edge Books, and manages Bridge Street Books in Washington DC. Smith edited *The Selected Letters of Robert Creeley* (U. Cal., 2014) with Peter Baker and Kaplan Harris. He has taught writing at the Corcoran College of Art & Design, George Mason University, and The Iowa Writers' Workshop, and currently teaches at The Maryland Institute of Contemporary Art.

JULIANA SPAHR edits the book series Chain Links with Jena Osman, Subpress with nineteen other people and Commune Editions with Joshua Clover and Jasper Bernes. With David Buuck she wrote *Army of Lovers*. She has edited with Stephanie Young *A Megaphone: Some Enactments, Some Numbers, and Some Essays about the Continued Usefulness of Crotchless-pants-and-a-machine-gun Feminism* (Chain Links, 2011), with Joan Retallack *Poetry & Pedagogy: the Challenge of the Contemporary* (Palgrave, 2006), and with Claudia Rankine *American Women Poets in the 21st Century* (Wesleyan, 2002).

FAKHAIR SPENCE chose not to provide a biographical note.

MOEZ SURANI's writing has been published internationally, including in *Harper's Magazine*, *The Awl*, *The Walrus*, *Best Canadian Poetry 2013* and *Best Canadian Poetry 2014*. When his first collection of poetry, *Reticent Bodies*, was published, one critic assessed the book's impact: "*Reticent Bodies* is that rare book that has the power to be a lynchpin, a hinge in the history of Canadian poetry." In 2012, Surani published a second collection, *Floating Life*, which was described as suffused with "stunning, simple images." His third book, "عملية *Operación Opération Operation* 行动 Операция, which is comprised of military operation names from UN-member states, will be published by BookThug in the fall of 2016.

KO KO THETT is a poet by choice and Burmese by chance. *The Burden of Being Burmese*, a collection of ko ko thett's poems that have appeared in literary journals worldwide, was published by Zephyr (Hong Kong and US) in 2015. He has recently read at Sharjah International Book Fair, Hong Kong Poetry Nights and Minsheng Art Museum in Shanghai. After a whirlwind tour of

Southeast Asia and Europe for about 18 years, ko ko thett is now happily re-settled in Yangon. He writes in both Burmese and English.

EDWIN TORRES came to poetry through performance art in New York City's East Village in the early '90s. The neighborhood's diversity plus the combined forces of Dixon Place, The Nuyorican Poets Café, and The St. Marks Poetry Project, shaped his multi-disciplinary approach to language. His books include, *Ameriscopia* (University of Arizona Press), *Yes Thing No Thing* (Roof Books), and *The PoPedology Of An Ambient Language* (Atelos Books). Fellowships include; NYFA, The Foundation for Contemporary Performance Art, The DIA Arts Foundation and The Poetry Fund. Anthologies include: *Angels of the Americlypse: New Latin@ Writing, Post-Modern American Poetry Vol. 2,* and *Aloud; Voices From The Nuyorican Poets Café.*

RICHARD TUTTLE (b. 1941, Rahway, New Jersey) is one of the most significant artists working today. Since the mid-1960s, he has created an extraordinarily varied body of work that eludes historical or stylistic categorization. Tuttle's work exists in the space between painting, sculpture, poetry, assemblage, and drawing. He draws beauty out of humble materials, reflecting the fragility of the world in his poetic works. Without a specific reference point, his investigations of line, volume, color, texture, shape, and form are imbued with a sense of spirituality and informed by a deep intellectual curiosity. Language, spatial relationship, and scale are also central concerns for the artist, who maintains an acute awareness for the viewer's aesthetic experience. Tuttle was the Artist in Residence at the Getty Research Institute from September 2012–June 2013. The artist lives and works in Mount Desert, Maine; Abiquiu, New Mexico and New York City. Tuttle's most recent shows are "Critical Edge" at the Metropolitan Museum of Art in New York (2016) and "Both/And Richard Tuttle Print and Cloth," at Fabric Workshop & Museum, Philadelphia (2015), which was accompanied by a book for his poems relating to many of the works in the show.

IMANI UZURI is a composer and vocalist whose work has been called "stunning" by *New York Magazine*. She travels internationally, creating concerts, experimental theater, performance art and sound installations in venues/festivals including Joe's Pub, The Kitchen, Whitney Museum, Central Park Summer Stage, MetBreuer, Performa Biennial and MoMA (Museum of Modern

Art). *The Village Voice* says, "Imani Uzuri is a constant surprise . . . seamlessly combining jazz, classical, country and blues motifs into highly personalized compositions." Uzuri is currently composing a new musical *GIRL Shakes Loose* with book by playwright Zakiyyah Alexander (featuring the poetry of Black Arts Movement award-winning poet Sonia Sanchez). She recently premiered her first orchestral composition *Placeless* at Ecstatic Music Festival and was subsequently named by The *New Yorker* as one of the emerging "female composers edg[ing] forward." Uzuri was a 2015 Park Avenue Armory Artist-In-Residence and is currently composing her first opera *Hush Arbor* as a 2015 MAP Fund grantee. The *New York Times* has praised Uzuri's "gorgeously chesty ruminations." In Spring 2016, Uzuri marked her Lincoln Center American Songbook debut as well as her appearance as a featured performer on BET's *Black Girls Rock*. www.imaniuzuri.com

JACK WATERS is a filmmaker, performance artist, dancer and builder of avant-garde communities. His work has appeared in the Whitney Museum "Black Male" Show, and literally hundreds of venues. He is on the board of Allied Productions, Le Petit Versailles and MIX.

STEPHEN WINTER was born on June 18, 1969 in Chicago, Illinois, USA. He is a producer and director, known for *New York, I Love You* (2008), *Chocolate Babies* (1997) and *Jason and Shirley* (2015).

ELIZABETH WILLIS's most recent book is *Alive: New and Selected Poems* (New York Review Books, 2015). Other books include *Address* (Wesleyan, 2011), recipient of the L.L. Winship/PEN New England prize for poetry; *Meteoric Flowers* (Wesleyan, 2006); *Turneresque* (Burning Deck, 2003); and *The Human Abstract* (Penguin, 1995). She recently joined the Iowa Writers' Workshop.

MATVEI YANKELEVICH is the author of *Alpha Donut* (United Artists), *Boris by the Sea* (Octopus), and *Some Worlds for Dr. Vogt*, recently released by Black Square Editions. He is a founding member of the Ugly Duckling Presse editorial collective, teaches for the Writing Division of Columbia University's School of the Arts, and is a member of the faculty at the Milton Avery Graduate School of the Arts at Bard College.

Editors

A graduate of Harvard Law School and the Iowa Writers' Workshop,
SETH ABRAMSON is an Assistant Professor of English at University of
New Hampshire and the author of five poetry collections, most recently
Metamericana (2015) and *Thievery* (2013). His awards include the J. Howard
and Barbara M. J. Wood Prize of Poetry, the Green Rose Prize from Western
Michigan University, and the Akron Poetry Prize from University of Akron.

CHARLES BERNSTEIN's most recent book of essays is *Pitch of Poetry*. His
most recent books of poems are *Recalculating* (2013) and *All the Whiskey in
Heaven: Selected Poems* (2010). Bernstein is Donald T. Regan Professor of
English and Comparative Literature at the University of Pennsylvania, where
he is co-director of PennSound. In 2015 Bernstein was awarded both the
Münster Prize for International Poetry and Janus Pannonius Grand Prize for
Poetry. More info at epc.buffalo.edu.

JESSE DAMIANI was the 2013–2014 Halls Emerging Artist Fellow at the
Wisconsin Institute for Creative Writing and has received awards from the
Academy of American Poets and the Fulbright Commission. He lives in Los
Angeles.

TRACIE MORRIS is a poet, singer, critic, scholar, bandleader and actor. She
holds an MFA in Poetry from Hunter College, has studied classical British
acting technique at the Royal Academy of Dramatic Art in London, American
acting technique at Michael Howard Studios, is an alum of Cave Canem's
summer residency and holds a PhD in Performance Studies from New York
University. Her 4th collection of poetry, *handholding: 5 kinds*, was published
in 2016. Tracie is professor and Coordinator of the MFA program in
Performance + Performance Studies at Pratt Institute, Brooklyn, New York.